PROCLAMATION:

**Aids for Interpreting the
Lessons of the Church Year**

✦ ADVENT ✦
CHRISTMAS

SERIES A

**Samuel Wylie †
and
John L. McKenzie**

FORTRESS PRESS   Philadelphia, Pennsylvania

Table of Contents

COPYRIGHT © 1974 BY FORTRESS PRESS

Library of Congress Catalog Card Number 74-76924

ISBN 0-8006-4061-6

Second printing 1976

5898E76   Printed in U.S.A.   1-4061

General Preface

Proclamation: Aids for Interpreting the Lessons of the Church Year is a series of twenty-five books designed to help clergymen carry out their preaching ministry. It offers exegetical interpretations of the lessons for each Sunday and many of the festivals of the church year, plus homiletical ideas and insights.

The basic thrust of the series is ecumenical. In recent years the Episcopal church, the Roman Catholic church, the United Church of Christ, the Christian Church (Disciples of Christ), the United Methodist Church, the Lutheran and Presbyterian churches, and also the Consultation on Church Union have adopted lectionaries that are based on a common three-year system of lessons for the Sundays and festivals of the church year. *Proclamation* grows out of this development, and authors have been chosen from all of these traditions. Some of the contributors are parish pastors; others are teachers, both of biblical interpretation and of homiletics. Ecumenical interchange has been encouraged by putting two persons from different traditions to work on a single volume, one with the primary responsibility for exegesis and the other for homiletical interpretation.

Despite the high percentage of agreement between the traditions, both in the festivals that are celebrated and the lessons that are appointed to be read on a given day, there are still areas of divergence. Frequently the authors of individual volumes have tried to take into account the various textual traditions, but in some cases this has proved to be impossible; in such cases we have felt constrained to limit the material to the Lutheran readings.

The preacher who is looking for "canned sermons" in these books will be disappointed. These books are one step removed from the pulpit: they explain what the lessons are saying and suggest ways of relating this biblical message to the contemporary situation. As such they are springboards for creative thought as well as for faithful proclamation of the word.

The authors of this volume of *Proclamation* are the late Bishop Samuel Joseph Wylie of the Episcopal Diocese of Northern Michigan and the Rev. John L. McKenzie, Professor of Old Testament studies at De Paul University, Chicago, Ill. Bishop Wylie, the editor-homiletician, served as a

iii

at the University of Virginia and Brown University, Canon of the Cathe-
dral of St. John, Providence, R.I., Rector of the Church of the Advent,
Boston, Mass., and Dean of the General Theological Seminary, New York,
N.Y. In 1972 he became Bishop of the Diocese of Northern Michigan, with headquarters in Menominee. Bishop Wylie's untimely death
occurred on May 6, 1974 while he was visiting New York City. The
exegete, Father John L. McKenzie, is a member of the Society of Jesus
and taught Old Testament studies at West Baden College, a Jesuit semi-
nary in southern Indiana, from 1942-1960. He also taught at Loyola
University, the University of Notre Dame, and as visiting professor at the
University of Chicago before going to De Paul University in 1970. Father
McKenzie is the author of several books; most recently he published his
Old Testament Theology (1972). He is a former president of both the
Catholic Biblical Association and the Society for Biblical Literature.

Introduction

Part of the Advent theme belongs to all men of goodwill. During the Advent season the universal longing for peace, for the reconciliation of man and nature, for simple justice, and for the vindication of God's people is expressed in the Old Testament Lessons. In more specifically Christian terms the Second Lessons or Epistles call seekers to watch keenly and with hope for the victory of light over darkness, practicing self-control and patience while they wait. The Gospels call to watchful preparation illustrated by the ministry of John the Baptist. (Note that the Christmas season virtually begins on Advent IV).

It is easy to find secular parallels to the Advent vision: West Side Story's "Something's Coming and It's Gonna Be Good!" and "There's a Place for Us, Somewhere" create the authentic Advent mood that the lectionary suggests. The audience is pulled into the agony and hope of the singers. Mankind longs for peace both in the sense of safety and in the sense of well-being and goodness. Poets, playwrights and musicians can be cited with good effect. Advent is the season when Christians and all other people of goodwill can share each other's hopes and honor each other's dreams.

Hymns and anthems and preaching together stress the biblical idea of watchful, hopeful, creative waiting. Advent lends itself to interpretation by the liturgical arts and family customs. Advent wreaths, banners, and any other means the local artists and youth groups can devise will make the preaching more readily understood. It would be possible and desirable to have every part of Advent worship give the sense of the nearer and nearer approach of the moment of God's ultimate disclosure of himself in glory.

Since all the Old Testament Lessons are from Isaiah, a sermon on the first Sunday combining the themes of all four and containing some references to the prophet and his ministry would be appropriate (although the critical notes warn against assuming that all verses come from the same hand). If a biographical sermon is attempted, subsequent sermons might focus on John the Baptist and on our Lord's fulfillment of the hopes of Isaiah and John. A series, Old Testament-based, examining the biblical grounds for peace, ecology (man's responsible partnership with nature) and public righteousness would be equally possible, but would run the risk of missing the Advent note of hope and coming breakthrough if the tone were too didactic. Another thematic series could emphasize Advent watchfulness the first week, hope the second, judgment the third, and the fulfillment of all three in the Christ-centered lessons of Advent IV. This latter would differ from a Christmas sermon by being chiefly concerned with teaching the significance of Jesus Christ in the plan of God and the fulfillment of men's hopes. The Christmas sermons would more logically celebrate his presence. Important in any series of sermons in this season is sufficient emphasis on our own share in the vision, our own longing for redemption, our own watchfulness for the signs of the Lord's coming. There is no encouragement in the lessons to identify Advent simply with preparation for Christmas. It is a season in which we learn to watch for impending glory. The idea of "glory" itself is an Advent theme. Angel choirs and Eastern sages suggest the element of wonder. The Old Testament Lessons provide models for political or social splendor, and the New Testament Lessons focus on the incarnation record or imply the glory of God shining in the face of Jesus Christ. From there it is only a short step to the contemplation of the reflected glory in the lives of holy people. Irenaeus said "the glory of God is a living man." David E. Jenkins' lectures *The Glory of Man*, and his preface to Moltmann's *Theology and Joy* develop the theme and are good preparatory reading.

The Advent themes tend to overlap throughout the season. For best use of the homiletical notes, read them through at a sitting and choose among some of the lines of thought suggested. You may find some of the material useful on other days than the one for which it has been offered.

The Navy calls its people to alertness and a readiness to hear and obey by calling "Now hear this!" over the loudspeakers. The servant of the Word has the most reason, perhaps especially in Advent and Christmas, to make a proclamation each week about the coming Kingdom and how to honor the King.

The First Sunday in Advent

Lutheran	Roman Catholic	Episcopal	Pres./UCC/Chr.	Methodist/COCU
Isa. 2:1-5	Isa. 2:1-5	Isa. 2:1-5	Isa. 2:1-5	Isa. 2:1-5
Rom. 13:11-14	Rom. 13:11-14	Rom. 13:11-14	Rom. 13:11-14	Rom. 13:8-14
Matt. 24:37-44	Matt. 24:37-44	Matt. 24:37-44	Matt. 24:37-44	Matt. 24:36-44

EXEGESIS

First Lesson: Isa. 2:1-5. Isa. 2:2-4 appears in Mic. 4:1-3. Modern critics are not generally inclined to ask in which book it belongs first; they rather believe that the passage is from neither prophet and was inserted into the two collections independently at a later date. The passage exhibits a type of future expectation which many interpreters think cannot be found in the second half of the eighth century, the period in which both Isaiah and Micah lived. The theme and tone of the passage are more akin to Second Isaiah, who wrote about the middle of the sixth century. It is possible to conjecture—but no more—that the scribes who added the passages in the two books thought of these lines as a response to Isa. 1:8 and 21 and to Mic. 3:12; this is altogether likely in Micah, where our passage follows immediately upon the threat of total destruction of Zion.

The first line, 2:1, is an editorial gloss or headline identifying the following three verses; the editor may indeed have intended the headline to cover the following material as well, in which there are ample references to Judah and Jerusalem. But his headline merely repeats the headline of 1:1, which suggests that he meant to draw attention to the "salvation saying" of 2:2-4.

The "latter days" (or "the end of days") became in later OT literature a technical term for the period which recent theology calls eschatological. That "the mountain of the house of the Lord" (Zion, the mountain of the temple) should become the highest of all mountains is an obvious poetic hyperbole, tempered somewhat by the fact that the poet's observation had probably not gone beyond Hermon (9,000 feet) or Lebanon (10,000 feet); it is a symbolic expression of the hope that Zion will become the center of the earth. The ingathering of the nations is a theme of Second Isaiah (45:14-25) and Third Isaiah (60:1-22).

The Mountain of the Lord (Zion) becomes for the nations what Mount Sinai was in the traditions of the exodus; it is the mountain of revelation. The words "ways," "paths," "law," and "word" are terms of the revelation of the Law. The word *torah* ("law," verse 3) originally meant instruction, then revealed instruction, the "Law," the whole corpus of revelation contained in the five books of Moses. The word is hardly used here in the sense of "Pentateuch" which it acquired in later Judaism (and in the NT). On the other hand, the association of "law" and "word" with "ways" and "paths" suggests a strongly moralistic view of revelation. The verse does not suggest the distinction between the *torah* of the priests and the "word" of the prophet which appears in Jer. 18:18. It appears that the lines come from a period in which the collection of moral and legal traditions defining a way of life was becoming the dominant idea of revelation.

The result of this revelation to the nations is expected to be universal peace. Yahweh, presumably through his law and his word, will be the arbiter of international disputes. That he will judge "between" the nations seems to be an explicit change from the common phrase "judge the nations," meaning punish them. A vision of universal peace with quite different imagery appears in Isa. 11:6-9. In both visions it is obvious that the prophet sees universal peace as arriving with universal faith in the sole divinity of Yahweh.

V. 5 has the word "walk" in common with Mic. 4:5, which is hardly enough to establish a relationship between the two verses; furthermore, this passage lacks Mic. 4:4. V. 5 is probably an editorial gloss added as a hortatory conclusion; it does in fact serve as a transition to the rebuke which begins in 2:6.

Second Lesson: Rom. 13:11-14. These verses are taken from the hortatory part of Romans, which includes chapters 12-15. Such hortatory sections are normally the last part of a Pauline epistle before the conclusion, and it is not surprising that they tend to run to type. The distinctive feature of this passage which makes it well adapted to the liturgy of Advent will appear in the exegesis. The same feature keeps it from being very well connected with what precedes and what follows in the text of Romans.

The "hour" (Greek *kairos*, opportune moment) and the "full time" (RSV, the ripe time) had a meaning for Paul and his listeners which the modern reader does not see on the surface. This opportune moment and ripe time when salvation approaches (v. 11) is the expected second coming of the Lord in glory, the parousia. That Paul spoke of this event as imminent and within the reasonable expectation of his congregations is evident from several passages of the epistles. He uses the theme elsewhere, as a motive for the believer to live a Christian life and to make himself ready for the coming of the Lord in glory as judge. For many centuries the church has applied this theme of Paul to the liturgical coming of the Lord in the commemoration of his nativity.

The imagery of night and daybreak certainly emphasizes the nearness of the event. Paul's use of the imagery of sleep and awakening is varied and inconsistent. He could hardly be reproaching the Romans for drowsiness in faith and morality, since he did not know them personally; thus the first use of the figure is neutral. The second coming is the dawning of a new day, the eternal day, to which every one will be "awakened."

Paul then passes from the imagery of sleep and wakefulness to the imagery of light and darkness, an imagery which has its roots not only in the OT but in the older religions of the ancient Near East. Paul's allusion to a war of light and darkness is paralleled in one of the documents of Qumran; but the theme is common enough and the terms are so general that no literary connection is indicated. Light is the element of divinity and of good, darkness is the element of evil and, in Jewish belief, of evil spirits. There is no explicit reference to demons here; the works of darkness are sins. Paul is probably using a homiletic commonplace here; as we have remarked, he had no occasion to read a reproach to the Romans as he did to the Galatians and the Corinthians. The casual allusion to the armor of light can be filled out from Eph. 6:11-13, more briefly in 1 Thess. 5:8. It seems to be, as we have suggested, a homiletic commonplace.

The wicked works of darkness are arranged in three pairs—another homiletic commonplace? The first four of these are the vices which are long known as "Roman" from literature and art; in fact, the four words mention what is depicted in a number of Pompeian frescoes. Both the art and the literature deal with such parties as typically upper class, which again suggests a commonplace; we have no reason to think that the Roman Christians were socially a cut above the Corinthians (1 Cor. 1:26). The fifth and sixth words, however, designate more specific anti-Christian vices, which attack Christian love.

"To put on Christ" appears also in Gal. 3:27. As commentators remark, it is synonymous with "incorporation into Christ." Whether putting on, incorporation, or rebirth is mentioned, the process has radical moral effects as Paul describes it. The desires of the flesh are in opposition to the indwelling spirit. In spite of the first two pairs of v. 13, the "flesh" is not to be taken in the restricted meaning which it has acquired in

Christian homiletics. For Paul the flesh is much more than sexual con-
cupiscence, and the third pair of v. 13 is just as "carnal" in Paul's mind
as the first two.

Gospel: Matt. 24:37-44. This passage follows Matthew's version of
"the Synoptic Apocalypse"; and the division at Matt. 24:37 avoids two
difficulties in the text. The first difficulty is the discord between Matt.
24:32-35, which seems meant to give clear signs of an imminent event,
and Matt. 24:36–25:13, which emphatically declares that the event is
unpredictable. The second difficulty is found in 24:36, which seems to
deny to Jesus knowledge which in traditional Christology he should have
had. The selection of this lesson not only removes these difficulties, but
also removes the implication that the second coming is imminent. What
remains is a conventional exhortation to Christian vigilance and pru-
dence. This conventional exhortation lacks the sense of eschatological
urgency which many NT passages have. Modern homiletics seems to have
found no theme which expresses an equally sharp sense of urgency. The
liturgical application of the passage is based on the recurring allusions
to the coming of the Son of man, applied to the nativity; but the coming
meant by the evangelist is the second coming, the parousia.

The theme of vigilance is illustrated by three examples; the first of
these is biblical, the others are drawn from daily experience. That the
deluge of Noah caught men by surprise is not stated in Genesis, but it is
clearly implied. The author does not refer even implicitly to the expansions of Gen. 6:5 and 13 found in Jewish apocryphal and rabbinical
literature, in which the wickedness of men is imaginatively portrayed.
It seems unlikely that the author was unacquainted with this type of
interpretation, and we may judge that it did not suit his purpose. The
words "eating and drinking, marrying and giving in marriage" designate
the ordinary activities of life, and do not refer to the sinfulness of ante-
diluvian man. The worst implication one can gather is that men went
about the ordinary business of life with no thought of the impending
catastrophe. It is not said that they have been warned, and there is no
hint that the author thinks of Noah as a "preacher of righteousness"
(2 Pet. 2:5). The emphasis falls upon the idea of the unexpected catastrophe. This does not imply that the author ignores the moral discrimination displayed in the catastrophe; this discrimination is stated in his
second example—of men and women engaged in the same activities who
are separated by judgment. In these pairs there is a moral difference
which is known to God alone, on the basis of which one person is "taken"
and the other is "left." The "taking" refers to the assumption of the

righteous into the clouds with the Son of man (24:31; see also 1 Cor. 15:52; 1 Thess. 4:16). Commentators point out that the passage has no hint of the resurrection of the dead; the second coming is presented as an imminent event of urgent concern to the living.

The theme of vigilance is sustained in the third example of the nocturnal burglar. One must not press details; the householder can prevent burglary by vigilance, but no one can prevent the second coming by vigilance. One can only be ready, as the needs and possibilities of each situation demand and permit. In this example the element of surprise nearly obliterates the element of moral discrimination; the householder is rather an innocent victim of aggression. The missing element is supplied in the parable of 25:45-51, not included in this reading. The author seems to imply that simple unawareness of the impending catastrophe, at least for those who have heard the proclamation of the gospel, cannot be innocent. It is a gospel theme that those who deal with this world and its activities as the ultimate reality commit a basic moral blunder. The direction of this and similar passages is not so much against human sinfulness, in the ordinary sense of the term, as against human unconcern.

HOMILETICAL INTERPRETATION

Spears into plowshares is the universal dream and the words are often quoted, but note that Isaiah makes universal peace conditional to the acceptance of God's authority. The lessons for Advent II and III are similarly balanced. It might be interesting to collect a number of the biblical references often quoted without their limiting conditions. "You shall know the truth, and the truth will set you free" is preceded by "If you dwell within the revelation I have brought, you are indeed my disciples; you shall know the truth . . ." Truth, freedom, peace as concepts or even as states of being are not ends in themselves. They are the consequences of a right relationship, and the relationship is the primary concern. A sermon on the price of peace, both personal and social, could use the First Lesson for the substance and vision of peace, the Second Lesson for illustrations of the personal demands made by a serious commitment to the cause of peace, and the Gospel for the necessary attitude of vigilance. Note that peace is finally made by the Peacemaker. Our Advent hopes gather around a person as much as they do about the blessed state of being he introduces.

The vision announced in the OT as coming to pass in the last days is supplemented by the Gospel's command to watch for the signs of the Lord's coming. The last days are always imminent. Those who link his return with particular current events are missing the apostolic insistence that any day and hour may be the moment when the last trumpet will sound. The reference to the flood invites comments on the judgment the Lord's coming brings. The triumph of peace (First Lesson) and light (Second Lesson) involves setting men and institutions straight, or of sweeping them away. How was it in the days of Noah with the rest of the community? Incredulity and cynicism about the Ark, certainly, and business as usual in spite of the signs of community wickedness. Then chaos and death descended. It is a familiar OT theme. Are there signs of the death of our own times that should be noted? Can they be noted without obscuring the fact that our message is primarily one of unrelieved condemnation? Who are today's ark-builders? How does an ark-builder differ from a prophet of doom? The confrontation of God's judgment is an awesome experience which may lead to new life. It would be unfortunate to use the Advent announcement of that majestic theme for mere scolding about the sins of church and state.

Watching for signs of the Lord's revelation of himself is the constant Christian attitude to life according to the Advent Propers, and the Christian style of life should reflect the detachment, the tentativeness about possessions and status, that waiting for the Lord's appearing naturally requires. Ark-builders view local social hierarchies and even economic development in a more cool and detached way than empire builders. As it was in the days of Noah . . . how was it with Noah, do you suppose?

Obviously, few of the things that gladdened the hearts of his neighbors or plunged them into fear or despair could occupy him. We must see him involved with the coming moment of truth; alert, awake, self-controlled. That is the picture the Second Lesson evokes. (Discussions of Noah's historicity are out of place on Advent I. Neither the defense of Noah nor apologies for using him as an example are appropriate when faced with so majestic a theme as the approaching END and how to prepare for the definitive encounter with God.)

The study of these three passages might lead to a sermon on *time* as the Bible speaks of it: "The last days" of Isaiah, the "kairos" of Romans, and the dramatic warning to be ready in Matthew have obvious connections. Every "right" time in the experience of Christians and of the church is a revelation of God, a preview of the ultimate disclosure. Every "right idea whose time has come" has power beyond ordinary communication. God's time is properly honored by anticipation or watchfulness before the disclosure and explicit obedience afterwards. We cannot temporize, stall, or postpone our response to the self-disclosure of God.

While the subject is not very suitable for preaching, the preacher's own preparation requires a point of view about time in relation to eschatology. The biblical language is futuristic although the future experience is anticipated now in the present because of the believer's relationship to Christ. It might be well to meditate and read a bit on the theme before tackling a series of Advent sermons.

The Second Lesson stresses the note of self-discipline as we watch for the fulfillment of the vision or the longing stated by Isaiah. The laziness induced by over-indulgence robs us of the ability to see the vision; to watch for the signs of the Lord's coming. The deeper lethargy caused by disillusionment and despair blinds us to any intuition of glory. E. B. Browning reminds us that only a Moses sees a bush aflame, other people stand around picking blackberries.

Both the Second Lesson and Gospel urge the believer to "stay awake" or "to watch." A sermon on the biblical meaning of wakefulness or watchfulness would be helpful. Illustrations from the excited, tingling expectancy of a child waiting for Christmas, of explorers watching for a landfall after a long time at sea without charts will give feeling to what might otherwise be a purely intellectual exercise. What experiences of life do we long for and slightly dread at the same time? These are likely to be experiences of judgment that prefigure the final judgment, the final revelation.

Lutherans who elect the alternate gospel, the Palm Sunday story, will stress the joy of anticipation this week and save the references to judgment for future weeks. Hosannah to the coming one is the theme. The consequences can be dealt with later!

The Second Sunday in Advent

Lutheran	Roman Catholic	Episcopal	Pres./UCC/Chr.	Methodist/COCU
Isa. 11:1-10	Isa. 11:1-10	Isa. 11:1-10	Isa. 11:1-10	Isa. 11:1-10
Rom. 15:4-13	Rom. 15:4-9	Rom. 15:4-13	Rom. 15:4-9	Rom. 15:4-13
Matt. 3:1-12	Matt. 3:1-12	Matt. 3:1-12	Matt. 3:1-12	Matt. 3:1-12

EXEGESIS

First Lesson: Isa. 11:1-10. There is some doubt among critics whether this piece belongs to Isaiah; the doubt arises from the mention of "the stump of Jesse," which may indicate that the dynasty has fallen. Not all critics find this convincing. But there is no doubt that in 11:10 the reading includes a verse which is an addition much later than Isaiah himself, located here in the book because of the catchword "root of Jesse."

The whole passage (vv. 1-9) describes the ideal king, an object of hope and not of experience. The messianic expectation of the NT and of Christianity rises from the conviction, expressed in this and other passages of the OT, that a scion of the dynasty of David would appear who would realize the high hopes and promises which were attached to this dynasty. This messianic hope certainly survived the dynasty of David, and the question raised above about the date and authorship of this passage has no relation to the interpretation of the passage. The king is a charismatic ruler, which means that the spirit of the Lord reposes in him. The spirit which inspires a man to leadership is found in the stories of the judges and of Saul, but the spirit rests permanently upon David. The six qualities became the seven gifts of the Holy Spirit in the Septuagint, which used two different Greek words to translate "fear of the Lord." The first two pairs refer to qualities of government, the last pair to religious devotion.

The student of the OT is struck at the contrast between the qualities of the king as judge and defender (vv. 3-5) and what he reads of the historical reality of the dynasty of David in the historical books and the prophets. The writer hopes for a charismatic insight which will rise above hearsay; after all, what is a legal process except critically examined hearsay? The judge will be favorable towards the poor—one might even say prejudiced; the judicial processes of the ancient Near East were usually weighted in favor of property. In 11:4 we should probably read "ruthless" as the object of "smite" (NEB) rather than "earth" (Hebrew text and most versions). The scope of the rule of the ideal Davidic king is not yet cosmic. The attributes of the ruler he shall wear as a garment; the figure does not suggest something superficial, for the garment mentioned is the most intimate garment of male apparel. Among the qualities of the ideal ruler are not included the virtues of the warrior; this sets this passage in contrast with Isa. 9:2-7, and it may be an additional reason, rarely noticed by commentators, for thinking that the passage is later than Isaiah. The only weapon of the ideal king is the spoken word; the same figure is used of the Servant of the Lord (Isa. 49:2), and it is applied to the exalted Christ in Rev. 1:16; 19:15.

The result of the reign is peace for the kingdom of Judah (not universal peace; "my holy mountain," v. 9, means Zion). Peace is a return to the conditions of Paradise, although the absence of predatory instincts is not explicit in Gen. 2-3. It may, however, be implied in the fact that the man gave names to the animals (Gen. 2:20); to confer a name is an act of dominion. Natural science is of no use in the interpretation of this text, nor is it accurate to call it poetic imagery. The Paradise of the beginning and of the end is a myth. The image of the land of Yahweh as an island of peace in a world of strife is also a myth. The "earth" (v. 9) is rather the "land," the land of Yahweh. Its peace is assured by the recognition of Yahweh.

We have noticed that v. 10 is an addition, the first of several added sayings. This looks not to Judah, but to the universal recognition of the messianic king of the future. This theme is better established in post-exilic prophecy than in the prophets of the eighth century. The scion of David is a new David who reestablishes the empire of David, extended far beyond the boundaries of David's empire.

Second Lesson: Rom. 15:4-13. This reading is selected from a longer passage which has as its main interest exhortations to Christian love and unity. This thrust is still apparent in the verses selected, though the selection as such tends to focus attention on the meaning of the OT for Christians. This is evident in v. 4, which candidly states the Christian thrust of the OT; indeed, Paul speaks as if the OT were written only for Christians with no direction towards the contemporaries of the biblical writers. Modern theology demands a much more nuanced statement of the relation between the OT and NT—a statement so nuanced that one agreeable to all churches and believers has not yet been produced. Without qualification the acceptance of this verse has left the church entangled in the wilderness of typology, prediction, foreshadowing and other forms of symbolism which attempt to make the OT mean things it never meant. Apart from these excesses, it remains true that the books of the OT sustain the Christian's patience and nourish his hope; and the God who is the author of these sayings is "the God of steadfastness and encouragement" (v. 5).

The first result of steadfastness and encouragement is that Christians should live in harmony with each other; and the sensible symbol of this harmony is religious unity, praise of God with one voice. Paul did not foresee the religious divisions of later centuries; the existence of these divisions takes nothing away from his conviction that Christian unity ought to have its symbolic cultic expression. A less symbolic and more realistic expression is "welcome" (v. 7), a word which means more than the conventional "welcome"; it means "to take to oneself," with no more discrimination than Christ showed toward the redeemed.

The major obstacle to Christian unity in the apostolic church was the division between Jews and Gentiles; this division has affected almost every book of the NT. Against this background the entire NT teaching on Christian unity was formed, and some of its expressions are strange to modern readers, to whom this problem of disunity seems unreal. Unfortunately, the principles implicit in Paul's treatment of unity are not always perceived by modern readers, who see no application of these principles to their own ethnic and religious divisions. Here Paul, writing for Gentiles, finds it necessary to justify the mission of Christ to Jews. Writing to Jews he found it necessary to justify Christ's mission and his own to Gentiles. For both of these arguments Paul recurs to the OT, according to his own rabbinical training; for this is the document in which God has declared his intentions. Christ had to go to the Jews to prove God's fidelity to the promises of salvation to his people which are so common in the OT. The mission to the Gentiles is justified by some exegesis which the modern interpreter finds strained—although a number of OT passages express clearly and without ambiguity the saving purpose of God for the Gentiles. Actually these are not the passages chosen here; these passages are chosen by verbal association. Interpreters believe that the passages were not chosen at random. The four texts represent the three major divisions of the Jewish Bible: the Law, the Prophets and "the Psalms," the third division which went by several titles. Thus Paul supports the mission to the Gentiles from the whole Scriptures. The principle of verbal association is also followed in modern liturgical arrangements; for the fourth text (15:12) is taken from the first reading for this day.

Gospel: Matt. 3:1-12. In all four Gospels the mission of Jesus is preceded and announced by the mission of John the Baptist. This mysterious figure has never been completely understood. A possible disagreement between the disciples of Jesus and the disciples of John (see Acts 19:1-7) has left no certain traces in the NT. In the Gospels, and especially in Matthew, John is the precursor of Jesus; he is Elijah returned (Matt. 11:14; 17:10-13). His garb and manner of life suggest Elijah (3:4; see 2 Kings 1:8). Like Elijah, his home was the desert, in no fixed abode. The location of John's activity in the desert of Judah has in recent years aroused speculations about a possible connection between John and the community of Qumran. Geography places him so close to Qumran that some association seems impossible to deny; but the literature reveals no assured relationship. All the Gospels attest the wide popular appeal of John (3:5-6; see also Matt. 21:23-27). All three Synoptic Gospels use

Isa. 40:3 to describe John's mission, surely a very early Christian attempt to solve the problems of the relationship of Jesus and John by the use of a fulfillment text. This was done by altering the sense of the Hebrew; the colon belongs after "crying", not after "wilderness."

That John is a precursor is clearly implied in close similarities between his proclamation and the proclamation of Jesus. Matt. 3:2 is identical with the words of Jesus in 4:17. Matt. 3:10 is very close to the words of Jesus in 7:19. Like Jesus, John criticized the religious leaders of the Jews; and the epithet "brood of vipers" is repeated in 12:34 and 23:33. As a preacher of repentance and of the coming act of God, John was easily accepted as a precursor; but his use of the rite of baptism caused some problems.

All the Gospels make some effort to distinguish between the baptism of John and the baptism of Jesus. Matthew omits the description of the baptism of John as "a baptism of repentance for the forgiveness of sins" (Mark 1:4) which is a designation of Christian baptism. Matthew himself distinguishes between the baptism of water and the baptism with the Holy Spirit and with fire (3:11). One may compare this again with Acts 19:1-7; the disciples of John had received baptism but not the Spirit. Yet in the following verses (not in this lesson) Jesus himself receives the Spirit in the baptism of John (3:13-17). The early Christian theologians had not achieved that perfect consistency for which their successors still strive.

The proclamation of John is strongly if vaguely eschatological. The threat of "the wrath to come" can be supported from Amos 5:18 and Zeph. 1:14-16; but Jewish apocryphal literature shows that the theme of the coming wrath had been much expanded in works contemporary or nearly so with the first half of the first century A.D. The threat that God could raise up sons of Abraham from stones, while not without parallel in the OT (Exod. 32:10), rather reflects the Christian belief that the true Israel were the believers in Jesus as Messiah.

John's proclamation of Jesus is also strongly eschatological. He is seen exclusively as judge, a role which he has in other NT books; but this role does not come close to describing him fully. Thus the Gospels, while identifying John as a precursor and giving him some words in common with Jesus, leave him a certain primitive quality which, we may be sure, reflects the historical reality of John.

HOMILETICAL INTERPRETATION

The ministry of the Holy Spirit is a central theme in all three lessons. While obviously not explicit in the OT passage, v. 2 of Isaiah in the

Septuagint is the basis for the listing of the seven-fold gifts of the Holy
Spirit at Confirmation in prayers such as the following from the new
Trial Rite of the Episcopal Church: "Strengthen and confirm them, O
Lord, with the riches of your Holy Spirit: an inquiring and discerning
spirit, a spirit of purpose and of perseverance, a spirit to know and to
love you, and a spirit of joy and wonder in all your works." Perception
and power underly this mention of the Spirit of the Lord and subsequent
verses show that these qualities are used to vindicate the wretched and
to bring down the ruthless. The Second Lesson concludes with a kind of
benediction, praying that the power of the Holy Spirit may remove all
bounds to hope, and the Gospel quotes John the Baptist as saying that in
contrast to his baptism signifying repentance, the more powerful coming
One will baptize with the Holy Spirit and fire. The relationship of the
Holy Spirit to the manifestation of God's glory could be an Advent theme
consistent with the hymns and customs of the season. Empowerment or
breakthrough are expressed or implied both in terms of social righteousness (First Lesson and Gospel) and of personal growth (Second Lesson).
Pentecostal or charismatic fellowships and those who seek to evaluate
them have material here on which to center.

The Isaiah passage, especially if combined with references to the First
Lesson for Advent III, lends itself to a sermon on man's stewardship of
nature, or the reconciliation between man and nature, and on the cosmic
aspect of Christ's redemptive role. We are accustomed to relating history
and ethics to Jesus Christ: now we are reminded from many sources of
his cosmic or organic role in redemption. Romans 8, citing nature as
waiting eagerly for man's redemption in order to find its own, is perhaps
the classic NT point of reference. Teilhard de Chardin and his disciples
and critics as well provide material for thought as do Irenaeus and the
poems and hymns of the Celtic saints. Jesus Christ's incarnation linked
God with the stuff, the goods, or the substance of creation. Such a sermon in the Advent season would present Jesus Christ and the kingdom
relationships he demonstrated, including those with nature, as a preview
of the ultimate state or condition when God is All in all. The note of
judgment in the Gospel and of hope in the Second Lesson can as easily
be applied to man's use and misuse of nature as to his treatment of his
fellows. It would be important not to preach a sermon on ecology, but to
preach on God's plan for man and nature drawing on ecology for
illustrations.

Unlike the treatment of hope in 1 Peter 1: 3—9, where the resurrection of
Christ is the sole basis for the believer's confidence, Rom. 15:4-13 relies
on the scriptural evidence of God's faithful help to those who refuse to

give up, and urges that the same friendly treatment be given to the brethren. Our hope is in the way God acts, including the way he acts through and among us. If Advent is treated as a time of pilgrimage and of waiting for the daybreak or the perception of a glory about to be revealed, mutual strengthening is in order. How God acts, definitively, is in the incarnation and resurrection of our Lord, and the promise of his coming, so both Romans 15 and 1 Peter are relevant to any treatment of hope. Some of hope's legitimate dreams are expressed in the OT lessons for the season: an end to war and want among them. The judgment that falls when the vision is rejected can be inferred from the Gospels, as well as the yearning, an almost visceral yearning for decency, righteousness and the knowledge of God. Here, especially, secular sources can be quoted to state the dream in an idiom familiar to this decade's hearers. Winston Churchill, John Kennedy, de Gaulle had the knack in political speeches. Modern folk music is as poignant and barbed at times as Amos and Jeremiah. Watch for current material to garnish and embody the perennial theme.

Some readers, remembering former lectionaries, may want to preach on the place of the Bible in preparation for the Lord's Advent. It will be hard from these pericopes to build up direct material for a teaching sermon on the nature and authority of Scripture, but it is possible from these lessons to preach on the Word of God, proclaimed by prophets and in scriptural testimony to God's faithfulness to his covenant, announced by John and appearing in flesh and blood among us in Jesus Christ.

A sermon on the eventual unity of all men is in order both to the Advent season and to the Second Lesson. Christians are called to perseverance on behalf of the weak, mutual help, tolerance, "following the example of Christ Jesus, so that united in mind and voice you may give glory to the God and Father of our Lord Jesus Christ." John and Paul identify visible Christian and human unity with God's glory. The bond of unity between Jews and pagans and among all men, is Jesus Christ, "who did not think of himself" (v. 3), the servant of Jews on behalf of Gentiles as well (v. 8). Christ as unifier of humanity is not presented as a dogmatic formula, nor is he used as one party's weapon against another. His credentials are his humility and servanthood, and they are also the credentials of his servants. The First Lesson can be included in the vision. A warning against the equivalent sin of saying "We have Abraham as our father" in our day is painfully apt. Any claim to faith, to morals, to order, to liturgy that is meant to put down someone else invites judgment. The fruit of all those good things is unity or a longing for it, and the humble offering of what one has to give. If "having Abra-

ham," or pure doctrine, or apostolic order, or high morality, leads us to
scorn for our brothers instead of love, we have not only missed the point,
we have misused God's gift to us in trust for all.

Today's Gospel and next week's provide two sides to the character of
John the Baptist. He is less formidable as in prison he fights his doubts
about the truth of his vigorous proclamation on behalf of the kingdom
and Jesus as the King. The man, his style and his message are revealed
in remarkably few words. Is he a typical herald of the age to come? Is
he a model for Christians in general? How essential was his style to the
credibility of his message? What about us? Can the church announce a
kingdom not of this world from the midst of worldly affluence? If in fact
you minister in poverty-stricken circumstances, are there advantages and
a kinship with both John the Baptist and his Master to be claimed? How
far would John the Baptist get in the ecclesiastical world of today? Are
there contemporary John the Baptists around us whom we ignore? Who
are they? John the Baptist contrasts his ministry to Christ's in terms of
power. What other contrasts come to mind?

"Prepare a way for the Lord" is a perpetual assignment for Christians.
Adaptation to change in the light of that assignment is a theme worthy
of meditation and a homily. As long as the status quo is obviously not
the Kingdom of God, we can expect the axe to be laid to the roots. While
Christians do not build each other up in hope, while hurt and harm are
far more characteristic of society than peace and well-being, the prophet's warning of doom to come and his call to the remnant who care to
repent and prepare a highway for the Lord are in season. Our traditions
are to help us discern the signs of the kingdom. They are not to insulate
us against the judgment. God can raise children for Abraham from any
available stones. How do we accept the historical comfort of the Scriptures mentioned in the Second Lesson without hardening it into the
insular and insulating pride condemned in the Gospel? Is not John's very
style of life a reminder to the church to remember its pilgrim status and
lay up its treasures in heaven, that is, to set even more store by what is
coming than by what has yet been revealed, and certainly to avoid en-
trapment in the questions of possessions and status that characterize the
present age or kingdom? If change and our response are central in the
sermon, a substantial minor section might deal with repentance.

Or, a sermon on repentance itself is consistent with the overall Advent
theme. As mentioned earlier, the other lessons indicate what is wrong
with us, and the Pharisees and Sadducees stand for our stiffnecked pride,
religious and national. The word repentance in both its Hebrew and
Greek senses is worthy of study: felt grief on the one hand, or, on the

other, rational substitution of a new course for the offending one. In God's mercy he does not require a single style of repentance; what counts is the about-face and the new commitment. Baptism into Christ or discipleship to Christ, is enablement, empowerment, the capacity to be a different person and the agent of a new community. Purging or cleansing by fire is involved: John the Baptist cannot imagine the casual conventional Christianity that emerged later. The reward of discipleship is a share in the coming kingdom and the privilege, now, of building a road for the coming king. If the discipline seems too tough at times, that is what the hope the Second Lesson speaks of is for, and that is why brothers and sisters give each other a hand.

The Third Sunday in Advent

Lutheran	Roman Catholic	Episcopal	Pres./UCC/Chr.	Methodist/COCU
Isa. 35:1-10	Isa. 35:1-6a, 10	Isa. 35:1-10	Isa. 35:6, 10	Isa. 35:1-10
James 5:7-10	James 5:7-10	James 5:7-10	James 5:7-10	James 5:7-10
Matt. 11:2-11	Matt. 11:2-11	Matt. 11:2-11	Matt. 11:2-11	Matt. 11:2-11

EXEGESIS

First Lesson: Isa. 35:1-10. This poem is judged by most critics to have the style and concerns of the collection of Second Isaiah (40-55). The journey which is the theme of the poem is the return from Babylon, the place of exile, to Jerusalem (see Isa. 43:19-21; 48:20-21; 52:11-12). This journey is imagined as a new exodus; the wonders of the first exodus are not only repeated, they are surpassed. In the first exodus Yahweh provided food and water for his people by miracles (Exod. 16:1–17:7; Num. 11:4-34; 20:2-13). In the new exodus Yahweh regenerates the desert, turning its arid parched land into well watered meadows, rich with vegetation. The transformation of the desert is a favorite theme in Second Isaiah (41:17-20; 43:19-21; 44:3; 48:21; 49:9-10; 51:3). There is a basis in reality for this image. Normally after the meager winter rains of the desert regions there is a brief but colorful blossoming of grass and wild flowers. It endures only a couple of weeks, and is elsewhere in the Bible a symbol of the brevity of life (Matt. 6:30). Here it is a symbol of the return of life.

Some of the texts cited above deal with the regeneration of Palestine, most with the regeneration of the route of the desert journey. Very probably a difference is implied. The regeneration of Palestine is permanent.

The regeneration of the desert prepares the way for Yahweh who travels with his people as he traveled with them in the pillar of cloud and the pillar of fire in the first exodus. This is not a permanent regeneration of the desert; the desert bursts into bloom at the approach of Yahweh and returns to its natural aridity after he has passed. The vegetation is like a processional carpet which is laid down and rolled up. It makes manna from heaven and water from the rocks unnecessary. The desert is turned into the generously wooded areas of the mountains of Lebanon and Carmel and the coastal plain of Sharon.

To the regeneration of the desert there corresponds a physical regeneration of the people. It is not merely disease but the permanent crippling afflictions—blindness, deafness, lameness, dumbness—which are cured. It is unlikely that these are symbols of moral defects. The lines rather express a simple belief that it would not be much of a salvation if any of the saved were prevented from enjoying it by these afflictions. Second Isaiah (40:29-31) sees the impending fulfillment of hope as lending strength and endurance to the weak and the weary. It is the final burst of strength of the athlete who sees that victory is within his grasp.

V. 7 is unintelligible in the Hebrew and all translations are conjectural restorations; but the sense of the whole passage is not seriously affected. The route is not only paved with grass and flowers, it is also protected from predatory beasts. The exclusion of unclean and fools seems to refer to the redeemed people; one expects an allusion to protection from bandits, but this would be a strange way to speak of them. Some commentators see an allusion to the restoration of the conditions of Paradise. Far more obvious is the allusion to "the Sacred Way" of Babylon, a processional avenue on which the images of the gods were carried at great festivals. Yahweh creates such an avenue for himself in the desert, and his people are his fellow-travelers.

The wearing of everlasting joy upon the head is a figure based on reality. The wearing of wreaths or garlands upon the head as a cultic symbol of festal joy is widespread. The same practice in secular ceremonial was used in ancient times, and survives in many modern cultures. V. 10 is repeated in Isa. 51:11, where its originality is very doubtful.

Second Lesson: James 5:7-10. This passage deals with the Advent theme of the coming of the Lord. The technical term for the second coming, parousia, occurs in vv. 7-8. The passage is a response to 5:1-6, an invective against the rich who oppress the poor. These are threatened with "the last days"; the word parousia is used by James of this day of judgment. After this invective the author turns to those to whom he writes, obviously not the "rich"; they are the oppressed poor who have put their faith in God. Commentators have long noticed that James does not speak of the Christ event, the redeeming death and resurrection; and some have wondered whether the coming of the Lord in this passage does not refer to the Day of the Lord mentioned in some of the prophets (see Amos 5:18-20). Other commentators see in this passage one of James's rare allusions to a clearly Christian belief. Outside of vv. 7-8, "the Lord" in this passage is not the Lord Jesus but the Father.

The rich are threatened with wrath; the poor are exhorted to patience. The verbal force of 5:8 expresses the nearness of the parousia as clearly as any of the words of Paul; but the exhortations to patience seem to imply that the believers must be ready for a delay. The author seems to have retained the words of the early Christian proclamation; he does not modify them, but adds an exhortation which implies that they should not be taken too literally. One gets the impression that the author wrote at a time when, if the words of the early proclamation were taken literally, the parousia should already have occurred. If this is the correct interpretation of the exhortations to patience, it supports the critical opinion that the Epistle comes from the latter part of the first century at the earliest.

The author gives three examples of patience, of which only two are included in the liturgical reading. The first example is that of the farmer who must await the harvest. The example is not biblical, but the author uses the biblical phrase "the early and the late rain" to give the example a biblical tinge. The early rains occur at the beginning of the rainy season (October-November) and the late rains at its end (April-May); failure at either end of the rainy season means a serious deficiency. The example is not perfect; the farmer must be patient, but he expects an event which will certainly occur at a definite time. The patient expectation of the parousia is directed towards an unscheduled event. Between the first and the second examples the author interposes an exhortation against quarreling (v. 9); the exhortation is given an eschatological emphasis with its reference to the judge who is standing at the doors. Here again there is a phrase which suggests imminence rather than a distant event. The phrase "at the doors" is used of the imminence of the eschatological event only in the Synoptic apocalypse of Matthew (24:33) and Mark (13:29); it may have been a commonplace in the early proclamation.

The second example of patience (with "suffering" added) is the prophets. Similar allusions are found in Matt. 5:12 ff.; 23:29-31; Acts 7:52. Outside of the hostility shown towards Jeremiah (and his life was spared), there are no biblical instances of persecution of the prophets except the murders of Uriah (Jer. 26:20-23) and Zechariah (2 Chron. 24:20-22).

There were prophetic legends current in Judaism, some of which have been preserved, which furnished additional material on this topic. The liturgical selection strangely omits Job (v. 11), the proverbial example of patience.

Commentators wonder why the author did not include Jesus as an example of patience, as he is cited in 1 Pet. 2:21-24. It is true that James lacks a specifically Christian tone; Jesus is not mentioned after the title except in 2:1, and specifically Christian doctrines do not appear. But it is possible, as many have noticed, that James did not regard the suffering of Jesus as exemplary; it was unique.

Gospel: Matt. 11:2-11. The proleptic mention of the imprisonment of John the Baptist is not explained by Matthew until the narrative of John's death (14:1-12). The question of John is best understood as sincere; theories that it was a theatrical question intended to elicit an open messianic profession arose from a devout unwillingness to concede that John could have been uncertain about the messiahship of Jesus. The term "he who is to come" seems to be a technical messianic designation; it is, however, unattested in any Jewish source. The answer of Jesus is a chain of biblical quotations (Isa. 29:18-19; 35:5-6; 61:1). The raising of the dead appears in none of these texts; found both in Matthew and in Luke, it was added by Q, replacing the liberation of captives in Isa. 61:1. The principle of the catchword is used in this liturgical selection of texts; Isa. 35:5-6 is part of one of the readings for this Sunday. The answer is not a frank claim of messiahship, but it mentions phenomena which in the OT and Judaism were expected in the messianic era. In the Gospel of Matthew these phenomena are narrated in chaps. 8-10. Luke, who has a different arrangement, was forced to introduce them into this scene (Luke 7:21). The texts, however, do permit the discerning hearer to see a kind of messiahship which is not an eschatological judgment of wrath nor the establishment of a messianic empire over all the nations. It is a messiahship of "saving," in both Greek and Hebrew the word which we translate "save" also means "heal." Thus the text is an effective disclaimer of eschatological or political messianism reflected in much contemporary Jewish literature. It is also reflected in some passages of the NT; the Christians of the first century did not reach a perfectly consistent pattern in their belief in Jesus as Messiah.

The passage then goes on to the authentication of John delivered by Jesus. The uncertainties of the relations of Jesus and John were resolved in the Gospels by the definition of John as the precursor. The first virtue affirmed of John is prophetic firmness and independence of influence.

The second virtue is the austerity of life fitting to a prophet; John is else-where likened to Elijah (3:4). Interpreters suggest that the verse may also be a denial of royal messianism; the King Messiah does not send precursors clothed in rough garments. John could not be identified sim-ply as another prophet. In Jewish belief prophecy ended with the closing of the prophetic canon. This canon ends with the announcement of the messenger who prepares the Lord's coming (Mal. 3:1); John is identified here with this eschatological messenger. In the same Book of Malachi is announced the return of Elijah at the beginning of the last days (Mal. 4:5). John is therefore more than a prophet; he is the messenger of the coming of the Lord, and in him is fulfilled the announcement of the return of Elijah (see Matt. 17:10-13; Mark 9:10-13).

John is thus the greatest of men; but he is clearly placed under the old covenant. The new covenant inaugurated by Jesus so far surpasses the old that the least in the new is superior to the greatest of the old. One may compare the words of John 14:12 that the believer will do works greater than the works of Jesus himself. The verse is not intended to be a depreciation of John any more than John 14:12 is intended to be a depreciation of Jesus. John declared the arrival of an event, a saving act of God greater than all his saving acts in the past. In this event John had no share, and it is some measure of the magnitude of the event that it throws even John into its shadow. The line also has a direction to any surviving disciples of John who have not yet believed in him whom John announced.

HOMILETICAL INTERPRETATION

The First Lesson invites nature and man to welcome God's coming judgment and to enjoy a partnership that makes for productivity and peace. Judgment as good news, however painful the process, is part of the Christian message. Truth sets men free, light causes growth, fire purges, destroying only what is false: these are Christian statements about judgment. When we run towards our judge rather than away from him, we find, as in Isa. 35:4, that he is our savior. He destroys not us but what threatens our being. Yet it is against our nature to seek out the judgment. From Adam and Eve hiding in the garden to our own chil-dren hiding the evidence of their small offenses, mankind runs from the moment of truth rather than toward it, especially when guilty. Advent sermons on judgment must point out the different end God has in view in dealing with those who plead guilty, and the role of truth in healing rather than in destruction. The Christian is commanded to look toward the End, the final showdown, with joy, not because his works can bear scrutiny, but because the redeeming process leads beyond the recognition and abandonment of evil to new life. Judgment has as its goal a result similar to trash collection or garbage disposal; the freeing rather than the condemnation of the one who accepts it.

The Savior-Judge is a biblical theme worth expanding. It is partially illustrated in today's Gospel. John the Baptist, in last week's reading, announced one who would come to thresh the wheat and burn up the chaff. This week, Jesus in answer to John's question, says that sight to the blind, wholeness for all, Good News for the poor are the signs of his messiahship. It is a different concept: no wonder John was confused. The theme could be developed further in terms of authority exercised in service: Philippians 2:5-11, Mark 10:42-45, as well as the suffering servant chapter of Isaiah. The judge undergoes the sentence (Romans 3:21-31). If a copy of Dorothy Sayers' play, *The Just Vengeance*, is on hand, it could be useful in bringing out the drama of the discovery that our final helpless acceptance of judgment makes possible the revelation of the identity of the Judge, Christ the Savior. Something of the same import comes in Revelation where John turns to look for the Lion of Judah and sees—a lamb.

Are you the one, or do we wait for another? It is a reasonable question to put to Jesus Christ. If he *is* the one, suffering is worthwhile, and waiting (cf. the Second Lesson) is bearable. John's criteria were different from those of Jesus, as we have seen. What are ours? Jesus invites John to take a pragmatic view. Wholeness and worth have been conferred (not just offered); healing and good news to the disinherited have been received. The action is personal and social and non-political in a way that the politicians found dangerous. Clearly Christ's kingdom is not of this world, because the guidelines are totally different. But is his non-political kingdom any more compatible to this world than if he were proposing a political program? Christians who do not compromise the vision or the style are "signs of contradiction" (in Taizé's terminology) and appear to be about as "politically unreliable" to repressive governments as political activists. What do we look for in Christ and what does he value in us? How do we prepare a highway for that kind of a King?

While we are at it, what are we to expect from prophets? Obviously not sleekness, according to Jesus. Variety is possible. A subsequent paragraph in the same chapter indicts the people for accepting neither John's austerity nor our Lord's conviviality. It does appear, however, that a prophet is to be part of his message. Recall some of the exploits of Jeremiah, Amos, and Hosea for "signs of contradiction" fortifying prophetic words. It would be interesting to reflect on the proper balance between dogma and demonstration. Any knowledge of the predominantly European idea of a ministry of "presence" will be useful here. To be "present" to God and "present" to men is the disciple's assignment following the Lord's example. How did Christ do that? And how do we? Jacques Ellul calls Christians "men of the eschaton." We judge the world by a truth that is coming and which even now is more real than the reality we recognize around us. We are here to demonstrate that reality more than to talk about it.

The Second Lesson this week reminds us that waiting is as important as watching. The time schedule for redemption is in God's hands, not ours. We do not initiate: we watch and we serve when given the opportunity: we cooperate with grace. Meanwhile we wait aided by the same grace. Patience and hope are essential parts of the Christian life style. Overenthusiasm, manufactured excitement, frenzy are as bad as laziness and sloth.

If the sermons this season have tended to be hortatory or judgmental, this is the day to stress the heroism involved in simple endurance and trust under adversity. John the Baptist's agonized question is natural, but more creditable and grace-filled is the attitude, "Take what he gives and serve him still through good or ill who ever lives."

Somewhere in the Advent season it is well to address the solitary and the suffering for whom conventional Christmas family joys are unlikely or impossible. It is curious that the popular celebration of Christmas tends to exclude the very people who most share our Lord's lonely and pain-conscious experience. They will appreciate the consideration and today's pericopes give the occasion to commend their patience and to reiterate the fact that Christ's ministry was particularly for and among them. Note that physical healing is part of the OT picture of the attendant circumstances to the King's triumphal entry. Joy at his coming is to be universal and the disadvantages are singled out specifically for restoration in order that they may fully share the festival. Any Christian celebration of Christmas tailored by its style and perhaps by the hour of service to the hardiest, most convivial and least burdened misses the point. Preaching at Christmas time can over-emphasize family joys. The King himself is concerned with the faint-hearted and the weary. Jesus answered John's expectations by pointing to the exaltation of the broken people as a sign of his messiahship. Technology's demand for efficiency and Darwin's principle of natural selection do not apply in the kingdom of God.

In that connection the Second Lesson's invitation to patience and forbearance is moving. Relief from suffering is as imminent as judgment. The exaltation of the meek is as certain as the downfall of the unrepentant mighty. We watch for the signs of deliverance. With big stakes, cosmic stakes on our minds, we care less about our own disappointments and we have no time at all to bicker among ourselves.

While such a sermon is most effective addressed directly to those featured in the lessons (the broken, the meek, the uncomplaining) it could include practical suggestions to the strong and the wealthy about how the local community could profit by a Christ-like involvement on behalf of the handicapped and lonely. The Third Sunday in Advent provides good timing for the lonely to gird themselves for the holiday pain and for the fortunate to help overcome it.

Just as hope is assisted by mutual thoughtfulness and help (last week's Second Lesson), so patience is aided by forbearance. Complaints against the brethren are inconsistent among those who wait for the Lord's appearing.

The Fourth Sunday in Advent

Lutheran	*Roman Catholic*	*Episcopal*	*Pres./UCC/Chr.*	*Methodist/COCU*
Isa. 7:10-14 (15-17)	Isa. 7:10-14	Isa. 7:10-14	Isa. 7:10-15	Isa. 7:10-15
Rom. 1:1-7	Rom. 1:1-7	Rom. 9:1-5	Rom. 1:1-7	Rom. 1:1-7
Matt. 1:18-25	Matt. 1:18-24	Matt. 1:18-25	Matt. 1:18-25	Matt. 1:18-25

EXEGESIS

First Lesson: Isa. 7:10-14. This selection may be the most difficult passage of the entire OT, and it is only fair to warn the reader that little can be proposed as certain. One thing on which modern interpreters would agree is that the passage is not a prediction of the virgin birth of Jesus. Another thing is that the oracle of Isaiah was addressed to Ahaz of Judah during the war with Israel and Damascus of 736-734 B.C. known as the Syro-Ephraimite war. There agreement ends. The occasion was probably not the same as the sayings of 7:1-9, but the general historical context is the same. The Immanuel oracle proper is probably confined to vv. 10-17; 7:18-25 appear to be detached sayings placed here because of verbal association.

In the situation of the Syro-Ephraimite war Isaiah had announced that the will of Yahweh was political inaction (7:4-9). The announcement is fortified here by the offer of a "sign" like those given to Moses (Exod. 4:1-9) and Gideon (Judg. 6:17-24 ff., 36-40). Both of these were given in response to a request; only in Luke 1:20 is the request for a sign punished as incredulity. The offer of Isaiah was bold, but quite within the biblical traditions of signs, as in the examples given.

The sign of Isaiah is probably both the birth and the name. The name, "god is with us," is a profession of the faith which Ahaz by his secular politics has implicitly denied. The identity of the woman and the child is simply unknown, and space is lacking here even to recite the suggested identifications. The Hebrew word *almah* means "girl," much as we use the word, not "virgin." An *almah*, like a "girl," may be married or single. One text from Ugarit suggests that Isaiah may have parodied the formula of the announcement of a royal son; this must remain uncertain. Many think that the birth announced was the expected delivery of a son of Ahaz. There are not insuperable chronological difficulties in identifying this child with Hezekiah, the successor of Ahaz. In this hypothesis, with or without Hezekiah, the birth of an heir who carries on the dynasty is a sign that Yahweh is still with the dynasty in spite of the unbelief of Ahaz.

Interpreters have remarked that in any hypothesis, the sign of Immanuel (including everything up to v. 17 included) is an announcement both of deliverance (imminent) and of disaster (remote) for Judah. The early years of the child are correlated with both the deliverance and the disaster. The deliverance is based on the promises of Yahweh to the house of David, the disaster is a punishment for the unbelief of Hezekiah.

The "curds and honey" of 7:15 are nearly as mysterious as the identity of the child. The routine biblical description of the promised land as a land "dripping milk and honey" does not support the view that milk and honey were foods of scarcity; and in the context of 7:15, the child will eat these foods when the enemy has been utterly defeated. The added saying from a different hand in 7:21-22 does play on the phrase; there will be plenty of milk and honey (but no bread and meat).

Second Lesson: Rom. 1:1-7. This passage is an expansion of the normal introduction to letters in Roman times, which ran: "A to B, greetings." Such expansions appear in all of Paul's letters, but this is the longest. The first six verses identify Paul, the seventh the receivers. In identifying himself Paul gives a packed summary of his theology of redemption. When the letter was read to the Roman congregation, one is compelled to imagine that the congregation, which did not know Paul personally, must have been more than slightly bewildered.

The use of the English "servant" instead of the English "slave" helps little. In ancient monarchies, Hellenistic as well as Oriental, and in the Roman empire personal slaves of the ruler enjoyed his closest confidence. Paul's use of the word expresses his own belief that Christ has entrusted him with the most delicate and confidential mission. To this he is not only "called" but "set apart"; consciously or unconsciously, Paul echoes his own words in Gal. 1:15, which in turn echo Jer. 1:5. The "good news of God" was promised through the prophets, but Paul does not mean to limit the word to the canonical books of the prophets. It was a basic Christian belief from the beginning that the Christ event was the climax of a divine plan of salvation which began with creation.

The Christology of vv. 4-5 is in one way primitive, in another way notably advanced for a date near A.D. 57-58. As in Gal. 4:4, Paul insists on the authentic humanity of Jesus, and adds here his Davidic descent. Paul has created trouble both for systematic theologians and for exegetes by the use of the word which in the RSV is translated "designated." The Greek word means "limit" or "define." Orthodox Christology rejects the adoptionism implicit in such paraphrases as "constituted" or "appointed." Other Greek words known to Paul would be better for "revealed." It seems preferable to take the word as meaning "defined" in the sense of "known without doubt" and to take "in power" with "Son." The resurrection is always for Paul the convincing manifestation of the sonship of Jesus; it is the supreme work of power, the attestation of the sonship and lordship.

The antithesis between "according to the flesh" (v. 3) and "according to the spirit of holiness" (v. 4) balances the humanity of Christ and his divine sonship. The spirit of holiness is not "the Holy Spirit" in the trinitarian sense; it is the principle of that "power" which is revealed in Christ in his resurrection. Always present, it appears in its fullness only when he is "defined" as Son by the resurrection.

It is from Christ that Paul has received his apostleship. The purpose of the apostleship is to bring about "the obedience which is faith." The other uses of "obedience" in Paul support this interpretation. The apposition thus defines faith as a commitment to a person of higher power; and such a commitment can be called obedience, among other things. The idea of faith is rich in Paul and cannot be defined by any single word.

Paul's mission is to the nations (see Gal. 2:9); the language here certainly suggests that those whom Paul addressed were mostly if not exclusively Gentile Christians. They are called to be saints as Paul is called to be an apostle (v. 1). The formula "grace and peace" occurs in every one of the thirteen letters which bear the name of Paul. The two words are by themselves an expansion of the normal greeting, the one word "health." But Paul gives them a peculiarly Christian emphasis.

Gospel: Matt. 1:18-25. Modern interpreters recognize that the infancy narratives of Matthew and Luke are not history in any sense of the word. The interpreter must deal with that type of composition called *midrash*, a devout but imaginative reconstruction of events of which there is no authentic memory. For instance, the date of the birth of Jesus was not known, and still is not. Both Matthew and Luke agree that the place was Bethlehem, but Matthew knows of no journey to Bethlehem like that described by Luke.

V. 18 is somewhat misleading; the passage is not a narrative of the birth of Jesus but of the trial of Joseph. The narrative has as its purpose to affirm what Luke also affirms in his own way, that Jesus had no human father; he is the son of God. The betrothal (1:18) in rabbinical law had the juridical effects of marriage; infidelity was reckoned as adultery, the contract was severed by divorce, and the betrothed wife inherited from her husband. "Come together" means the actual wedding ceremony, accomplished by the husband's ceremonial taking of the bride into his house. The description of Joseph as a "just man" means that he was a zealous observer of the law; and the law was hostile to adultery. It is doubtful that the capital sentence imposed by the Levitical and the rabbinical laws was often imposed in NT times. The alternatives of Joseph were a public divorce, which would inflict public shame, or a private divorce. In Jewish law divorce lay entirely within the decision of the husband.

The problem of Joseph is solved by a dream revelation. It is noteworthy that dream revelations in the NT occur only in Matt. 1-2; 27:19 and in Acts. The angel of the Lord who speaks to Joseph is an OT figure who also appears in the infancy narrative of Luke, there with a personal name. "The Holy Spirit" (RSV) in vv. 18 and 20 is not entirely accurate; the word does not have the definite article in Greek. "A holy spirit" signifies a divine creative impulse; in Ps. 104:30 it is a principle of life. Commentators have noticed that the idea of conception without a male agent is entirely unprecedented in Jewish literature.

Matthew uses a fulfillment text (Isa. 7:14) which, by the principle of the catchword, is used in the first reading of the day. We noticed that "virgin" does not appear in the Hebrew text; but it does appear in the Greek version (*parthenos*), and this permits Matthew to employ it here. In fact the word *parthenos* does not always mean virgin in profane

Greek, and it is unnecessary to suppose that the Septuagint translators worked here with a Christian charismatic insight. They were, as they often were, careless. This does not alter the fact that Matthew meant to affirm a virginal conception and to support it by biblical evidence.

HOMILETICAL INTERPRETATION

Those who prepared the present lectionary were apparently aware of the growing tendency to celebrate Christmas on the Sunday before the Feast of the Nativity, or Christmas Day, itself, and have therefore provided essentially Christmas lessons for Advent IV. As stated earlier, the opportunity is thus given to prepare for the chief celebration of Christ's coming on Christmas by prior reflection on who he is. (Where Advent IV is actually the Christmas service, the propers and comments for Christmas Day are more appropriate).

The exegesis makes clear that the mystery of the incarnation cannot be proof-texted, at least from these lessons. The verses from Romans provide the only basis for an exegetical sermon on the doctrine of Christ. There, his humanity is clear and also his divine Sonship, though in an untypical line of argument. The resurrection is also cited in its central place for Christians as well as the universal claim on the obedience and faith of men and women that he extends through his apostle. In remarkably few and very theologically concise (and precocious) words Paul states the gospel, implies the church, and names Jesus Christ our Lord by his full title. A sermon entitled simply "Jesus Christ our Lord" could use those words to establish doctrine about his humanity, deity, and claims on all men. It would be important to identify the word "Jesus" with Joshua and to establish his genuineness as a human person as well as the Messiah (Christ) and Son of the Father. Probably Paul's identification of the revelation of Christ's divinity in connection with the resurrection would make more appeal to modern inquirers than the events suggested in connection with the virgin birth. To preach that latter doctrine as a logical sign of a divinity already observed makes better sense (and better follows the first century pattern) than to try to argue divinity on the basis of the virgin birth. Disciples were hungry for the stories of his birth and early life only after they knew and loved him. On that reasoning, the preacher might start with the word "Lord" and work back to "Jesus" and to "Christ". Evangelism was done by witness, and still is. Convincing testimony to the Lordship of Christ opens hearts and minds to the doctrine of his unique place in the history of God's dealings with man. That doctrine is supplemented by the story of Christ's full identification with a family and the human community in a particular place, and his identification with the eternal purposes and specific initiative of God.

Another frankly theological sermon could be based on Paul's apostleship. Isaiah, John the Baptist, and now Paul proclaim the revelation of God. Paul claims a personal relationship deeper than the other heralds, defines the gospel in terms of the person of Jesus Christ in whom the Kingdom previously announced is revealed, and calls all who hear and believe to the same relationship of faith and obedience that he himself enjoys.

A meditation on the Gospel could very appropriately involve imagination and fantasy put at the disposition of faith and love. Joseph may have been the first person but far from the last to be scandalized by direct involvement in a situation where God's purposes seemed to run roughshod over man's conventions. What will people think? is an irrelevant question where the preparation of the King's highway is concerned. Joseph was open to the correction of his conventional convictions. How far do angels (in whatever way God's messengers arrive) succeed in preparing hearts today? Why are some hearts responsive and others not?

The role ascribed to Joseph is one of protection, self-effacement and self-denial. "They also serve who only stand and wait." Popular awards, even in Christian reporting, overlook the necessary supporting cast. Let Joseph serve as a sign of the large number of invisible Christ-loving people who *do* their faith without explanations or applause. The presence of Christ in the parish is as much a result of their faithfulness as that of the public leaders.

Similar questions lead to speculation on the qualities of faith revealed by the blessed Virgin Mary. She said "Yes" to God, perhaps more deeply *was* yes to God; a response that we are also asked to make. She raised some questions for us about motivation and fulfillment in life. Self-realization, self-acceptance, have become a kind of gospel-language for us, and self-gratification or indulgence no longer sound wicked. Christian paths to self-acceptance, we are reminded at Christmas and Easter, include renunciation and obedience; both known to Mary and to Paul—and to Jesus Christ. Phil. 2:5-11 outlines the self-emptying, the humility, the degradation and the exaltation that make up the saga of our Lord's life. The theological language of Philippians is echoed in the poignant, gentle stories of Matthew and Luke.

Another way to approach the mystery of Christ as a climax to the Advent season would be to start with the secular images and questions that gather about him and to try to sort them out. What is the appeal of "Jesus Christ Superstar", "Godspell" and similar efforts? How do they correspond with the Gospels and where do they fall short? Why do some Marxists revere him and hate the church? Can the testimony of Jesus people and charismatics be identified with Paul's words in the Second Lesson?

Cardinal Suenens in a pastoral letter to his archdiocese quotes French Communist Roger Garaudy on Jesus Christ. Asked, as part of a survey by PARIS-MATCH, "What does Jesus Christ mean to you?" Garaudy replied:

"He has lit a torch.
He demonstrates the spark of flame that brought him to birth.
All wisdom before him meditated on fate, or necessity mistaken for reason.
He showed their folly, he the opposite of fate.
He, liberty, creation, life: he who defatalized history."

Any sermon attempting to define the ministry of our Lord should be rigorously tested before it is delivered. He came to bring hope, to set free, to expand horizons, to tell all kinds of men that God loves them, and to judge their works in the context of that good news. No sermon at all is better than one which seems to make the "brightness of the Father's glory" an advertisement for a particular church, the executive officer of an exclusive club, or a law enforcement officer. The preacher is on holy ground when he addresses himself to this theme. Necessarily the sermon must point beyond the limitations of its author, but also beyond the limitations of theology and Christian experience this far.

> Weak is the effort of my heart,
> And cold my warmest thought,
> But when I see thee as thou art,
> I'll praise thee as I ought.

The Nativity of Our Lord, Christmas Day

Lutheran	Roman Catholic	Episcopal	Pres./UCC/Chr.	Methodist/COC
Isa. 9:2-7	Isa. 9:2-7	Isa. 9:2-4, 6-7	Isa. 9:2, 6-7	Isa. 9:2-7
Titus 2:11-14	Titus 2:11-14	Titus 2:11-14	Titus 2:11-15	Titus 2:11-15
Luke 2:1-20	Luke 2:1-14	Luke 2:1-14	Luke 2:1-14	Luke 2:1-14

EXEGESIS

First Lesson: Isa. 9:2-7. Many commentators believe that Isaiah has modeled this passage after an accession poem employed in the ceremonial installation of a new king in Jerusalem. In this view the references to the birth of a child are not meant literally. They may be related to the adoption of the new king by Yahweh mentioned in Ps. 2:7; this psalm is also an accession poem. The birth of an heir, however, is normally celebrated in monarchies. Whether the poem reflects accession or birth, it attests the renewal of messianic hope at the acceptance of an heir or a new king. For the new king held the promises made to the dynasty of David, promises of eternal dominion and rule over an empire.

Isa. 9:2 presupposes 9:1; the two verses refer to the conquest of the territories of Zebulun and Naphtali by Tiglath-Pileser III of Assyria in 734-733 B.C. These territories were detached from the monarchy of Israel and incorporated into an Assyrian province. As these regions were the first portion of the land of Yahweh to fall under alien conquerors, so they shall be the first upon which the light of deliverance shines. The prophet can only have meant this as a poetic presentation, not as a historical prediction. The allusions to the deliverance are candidly military (as contrasted with 11:4), and the prophet alludes to the great victory of Gideon (Judg. 7). The oppressor meant must be Assyria, and the prophet does not expect an apocalyptic interposition of Yahweh. Judah will be delivered by its own prowess aided by Yahweh; what is promised is a holy war. This was not consistently the thought of the prophet, who elsewhere declares that Assyria is the rod of the wrath of Yahweh against his unfaithful people.

Government upon the shoulder is probably the key, the symbol of authority (see Isa. 22:22). The new king has four titles. Modern interpreters do not think that these titles are rhetoric. It has been proved to satisfaction that much of the court style of the Jerusalem monarchy was borrowed from the Egyptian monarchy. Each Egyptian king at his accession received his protocol, five royal titles which were added to his throne name. Many critics believe that there were originally five titles here; and this opinion is supported by the presence of two meaningless consonants at the beginning of 9:7 (9:6 in Hebrew) which could be all that is left of a fifth title.

The first title, literally "wonder of a counselor," cites one of the attributes desired in a king. The second title, literally, "god of a hero" (RSV "Mighty God") is slightly more difficult; it most probably should be paraphrased "Divine Hero." The word translated "hero" signifies a hero in war, again a desirable quality in a king. The third title, "Everlasting Father" (RSV), designates a quality of a king towards his subjects esteemed in the Near East as far back as Hammurabi of Babylon; if the title is paraphrased as "always father," the metaphysical implications which Christians read into the line are avoided. The fourth title, "prince of peace," states the desired effect of good government; "peace" is the condition of prosperity and security, both general and particular, which a king should secure. This is not achieved without "justice and righteousness" (9:7); these words generally refer to justice in legal processes, for the king is theoretically the judge of all cases in his kingdom. Finally, this condition cannot be achieved without "the zeal of Yahweh of hosts" (9:7).

Most commentators, we have noticed, believe that this passage is modeled after an accession poem. They have not seriously considered the possibility that it was an accession poem. The implication of this possibility is that Isaiah, who certainly enjoyed familiar relations with the king and the court, was himself a court prophet. If the poem is an accession poem, Hezekiah is the only king who can be considered as the king for whom the poem was written.

Second Lesson: Titus 2:11-14. The Pastoral Epistles (1-2 Tim. and Titus) are now universally recognized by critics to be products of the school of Paul's disciples and not of Paul himself; moreover, they are believed to be later in the first century, certainly after the death of Paul.

Titus is a moralistic epistle rather than a dogmatic epistle; the selection in this reading is a short dogmatic interlude in the middle of a series of moral exhortations which make up the bulk of the epistle. The selection is intended to give motives in belief for the moral obligations which the writer recites.

"The grace of God" which has appeared (v. 11) is Jesus himself. This somewhat abstract designation of Jesus is not usual, and suggests a later date for this epistle. This grace has appeared for the salvation of all men. This affirmation of the universalist scope of the gospel has no explicit reference to the Jewish-Christian controversy which is so prominent in most of the NT books, and seems to come from a time when this controversy was no longer a living issue. The will of God to save all men was at the time of writing an assured belief. The purpose of this "appearance" was moralistic (v. 12); this is the thrust of the whole epistle. The words rendered (RSV) "irreligion" and "godly" are direct contraries in Greek. Simple unbelief was, it seems, the prevailing state of mind in the Hellenistic-Roman world; when the Christian missionaries addressed Gentiles, they were not attempting to persuade them to change their religion but to adopt a religion. The phrase "worldly passions" is the only use in the NT of this adjective in the sense of the English "worldly." The three adjectives which describe the good life (v. 12) echo Greek philosophy rather than biblical language. This is clearly true of the moral ideals of "sobriety" and "godliness." "Godliness" or "religiosity" was esteemed as a desirable moral quality by almost all Greek philosophers, even those who were agnostics. It is probable, then, that the third quality, "uprightness," means the Socratic and Platonic ideal of justice rather than the biblical ideal of "righteousness" which the English word "uprightness" suggests.

The appearance of the grace of God is the incarnation; the appearance of the glory (v. 13) is the second coming. The sense of imminence is not obvious here; the author is more concerned with the effects of the incarnation in the present church. The titles of "great God and Savior" attached to Jesus Christ have caused serious problems to interpreters. Bible readers do not know that the ordinary Christian discourse about Jesus Christ departs notably from NT language, in which God is always the Father. This verse is clearly an exception, so clearly that some have questioned the text. There is no ground for this. The author does echo a phrase which was used in imperial acclamations. Interpreters generally think he was a Gentile Christian with no deep biblical background. The acclamation "great god and savior" was often applied to Caesar when he visited a city. Since the author is speaking of that triumphal coming which will outshine all triumphs, he made use, it seems, of the current language of such events.

The purpose of the redemptive self-oblation of Jesus (v. 14) is again seen as moralistic. Our hypothetical Gentile Christian author has a recondite allusion to the Septuagint in the word translated "of his own" (RSV), a word found only here in the New Testament. If it comes from Exod. 19:5; 23:26 and Deut. 7:6; 14:2; 26:18, it means not "his own" but a people which is a treasure. The author may not have known this. He probably did know that his language makes the church the new people of God.

Gospel: Luke 2:1-20. Of all the four evangelists Luke has invented most scenes which lend themselves to painting. A visit to any of the major collections of Renaissance art will demonstrate this. There is no historical basis for the legend that Luke was a painter, but his artless prose has created many word pictures. Of all these scenes none has been more frequently portrayed than the nativity of Jesus. It is necessary to recall that Luke's nativity narrative is as much an imaginative portrayal as any of the paintings which have been derived from it. Luke had no living memory of the nativity of Jesus with which to work. A comparison of his narrative with that of Matthew is itself enough to show this. One may choose either Matthew or Luke, but one cannot have both. In fact modern interpreters treat both as imaginative stories. The census which Luke makes the occasion of the birth of Jesus in Bethlehem creates insoluble historical problems; the evidence leaves no room for the hypothesis that it ever happened. Both Matthew and Luke were faced with the problem that Jesus of Nazareth was born in Bethlehem; each solved it his own way.

We deal with artistic symbolism in the service of belief, a kind of theology which we usually find only in art galleries. Yet only through the symbolism can we grasp the meaning of Luke. Luke is more than the other Gospels the Gospel of the poor. It is to the poor that the gospel is proclaimed and the poor are the first to believe it. Poverty as a virtue is more clearly and frequently preached in Luke than elsewhere. The nativity narrative is so contrived that Jesus is born near destitution. It is to the poor that the good news is first proclaimed, not to the wealthy and the learned. The proclamation of Jesus as Messiah in this passage, which has no later echoes, is premature; Luke intends to set the tone for the later proclamation. The heavenly messenger is a part of Luke's first two chapters; he is found in the birth narratives of some OT heroes such as Gideon, Samson and Samuel. But a whole angelic choir singing hymns of praise is found in the OT only in a few Psalm passages (Ps. 103:20; 148:2). This is a cosmic event, and it deserves cosmic recognition, even though it went unrecognized by the world of men. The RSV and most modern versions have abandoned the Authorized Version of the song of the angels for the critically superior reading. "Men of his good pleasure" taken by itself could be read as a piece of rigid predestinarianism.

The message of the angel is candidly messianic, more so than any of the words of Jesus himself in the course of the Gospels. The angel announces him in whom later Christians believed, whom his contemporaries did not recognize. The angel did not speak to them, we have noticed. He spoke to the lowly, for it was only the lowly who later recognized Jesus as messiah and savior. The word "savior" is used of Jesus only here in the Gospel and twice in Acts; elsewhere it is used in the Gospels only in John 4:42. It seems likely that this title of Jesus belonged in the Hellenistic preaching rather than in the Palestinian preaching; as a divine and imperial title it was common in Roman Hellenism, and Hellenistic Christians saw no impropriety in applying it to Jesus. "Christ the Lord" was an early designation which also seems to have been more at home in Hellenistic than in Palestinian Christianity. Thus the proclamation of the angel seems to have been couched by Luke in Hellenistic terms.

Twice in this chapter (2:19, 51) Luke refers to Mary's thoughtful memory of the events. This does not imply that Mary herself was Luke's source; in view of the historical difficulties of the narrative this is scarcely possible. It is possible, however, that Luke's sources associated her name with their material.

HOMILETICAL INTERPRETATION

As already mentioned and underlined, the principal Christmas service is a time to celebrate the presence of the Lord and to adore, to offer thanks, and to enjoy each other in association with him. There are better times to expound on the doctrine of the incarnation or to scold the present age for its commercialism, self-indulgence, etc. Similarly, if the preacher is concerned about the credibility of the birth narratives or is strong in their defense, or if he questions or strongly affirms the virgin birth and believes the pulpit is a suitable place for making his point, it has been suggested that Advent IV or the First or Second Sunday after Christmas would be a better time to do so than on the feast itself. Major feasts (perhaps also all Sundays) are times to bear witness: to affirm what we know, believe, or have seen done.

If the service is well attended by strangers and marginal Christians, the sermon will be a special but difficult opportunity to present Christ both as one now known and loved by some and potentially known by all. To make all who come welcome in his name, accepting a whole spectrum of response from adoration to friendly curiosity, satisfies the integrity of all present and frees the believing Christian to express his joy without putting his neighbor in a hypocritical position. All men of goodwill can be happy about the coming of Jesus Christ. Devout believers must also be given the opportunity to ponder, wonder and adore.

Preaching centered in what Christ has done for us may use the Second Lesson as the basic text with the other lessons as supplementary material. A meditation on the nativity story might supplement the Gospel by reference to man's hopes for deliverance focused in the First Lesson, and man's logical response to Christ's coming based on the Second Lesson. In any scheme using the three lessons, people will expect some reference to the Lucan account.

The First Lesson lends itself to meditation on God's gift to us. Deliverance and a deliverer are given. Light, plenty, and peace are the tangible gifts. They are given in a non-threatening way: a child, a boy. God gives power to use, but he does not overpower or smother us with his gifts. Moses, David, the Promised Messiah in Isaiah, and the babe lying in a manger all indicate a remarkable gentleness on God's part in the way he reveals himself. Joy in the coming of the Savior, and hopes in him and for him expressed in words like "in purpose wonderful, in battle God-like, Father for all time, Prince of peace" (NEB) are our response. The Second Lesson treats the terms of our response in greater detail. Perhaps a sermon on God's gift (First Lesson) and man's response (Second Lesson) would have value.

Note that the NEB equates salvation with health in this passage: God's grace brings healing for all mankind. The word grace needs to be made alive. Too many people think of grace as spiritual money, on the one hand, or, on the other, as a legal operation whereby God dismisses the indictments. God's goodwill, God's friendship as a means of saving health is gently demonstrated in the Christmas story. God comes, not in the expected pomp and power, but as a new child in the neighborhood, and in a stable at that. Vulnerable, trusting, emptied of all that might threaten us, God comes into our lives. This is grace. I remember a Marine major visiting an improperly ventilated hold on a transport in which a great number of seasick Marines were lying, helpless in their own filth. He issued no orders: they could hardly have been obeyed. He got a mop and pail and started to clean up. One by one the men found the strength to join him. Grace came for them with healing through the ministry of their battalion commander. Some such story, more locally based, may carry the meaning of the word "grace" to the Christmas congregation.

The grace that brings healing, the saving friendship of God, leads us to discipline which involves renunciation of godless ways and worldly desires (the value system of secular society) and to live the qualities of temperance, or responsibility, honesty and godliness. These qualities are the ones which cause Christians to be called "salt" or steadfast, to be good citizens, etc. They are not achieved by voluntary discipline. The discipline is the response in love to love. "The expulsive power of a new affection" is how the Scottish preacher Chalmers described the Christian concern with godliness. All of the Christmas devotion which centers around giving the Christ Child a gift has this solid and sobering backing. There is much material here to illustrate both the universal scope of God's gift of grace and the depth and manner of our response.

Note, also, that the Christian lives between the appearing of grace in the incarnation and the coming splendor, glory, denouement (v. 13). If the Advent theme of judgment and glory has been developed in previous weeks, this Second Lesson is an excellent chance to develop the idea of the "between the times" position of the Christian: halfway between the Red Sea crossing and the promised land, between the down payment on his inheritance and its possession. We look back to Christmas for the ground of our hopes and forward to the End for its fruition. A sermon using that theme can start with whatever gravely affects us on Christmas Day, this year, turning both to the grace that *has* dawned and to the happy *future* fulfillment of hope, calling for the kind of discipline expressed in v. 12. Although Christmas is hardly the day to develop it deeply, there is a theology of involvement and detachment here. We can name, support, back, all that works for peace, growth, and love without totally identifying salvation with any. For *that* we look back to the sign of Bethlehem, Calvary, and the Garden, and forward to the great clarification and glory.

The same framework provides for a meditation on simplicity; the simplicity of the divine "style" of salvation, simplicity of life on the part of Christ's disciples and the simple hope which tests and purifies the Christian's life-style. Pretention, pompousness, threats, and violence are not the road to truth or good government (of self, family, nation or church). Christ's knock on the world's door now is not imperious. But there will be a moment of truth of a different order later.

The Gospel story according to Luke will have been read and sung and visually demonstrated. To be heard with freshness, especially if it is the focus for the sermon, it should be read well, slowly and deliberately framed in the Service. Familiar lessons read poorly offend the hearers and make preaching difficult.

Note that the birth is described as a very simple event. The experience of the shepherds is a commentary on its meaning and in the Lutheran lection their subsequent visit to Bethlehem is a logical response. God acts, we perceive and then, in turn, take action ourselves. The promise of the angel is joy, joy in deliverance, joy for everybody. We have been dwelling on peace and saving health in Advent. Joy is something else, central to Christian faith, but often obscured or tamed in church by a joyless piety. Popular carousing (if truly joyous) may share more truly in the nature of the Christmas message than merely correct religious and social observances. But deliverance calls for the discipline of the Second Lesson as well: joy is productive, even though it is an adequate sign of Christian life in itself. The shepherds were receptive: Herod got something of the same word in the Matthew story but heard it as a threat. What makes the difference? What kind of person sees the splendor of the Lord and gets good news? Most people do not, certainly, in first century terms or modern ones either. It must say something about the impact of Jesus on those who first knew him either in the flesh or by faith that they felt that this kind of story was consistent with his life and message. They rejected many stories about him when the Gospels were written down: this story sounded authentic to them. If shepherds, and later fishermen and housewives were the natural company for Jesus, we must be sure that today's equivalent man in the street is told and comes to know that Jesus is his kind of person. There are no ecclesiastics in the Christmas story, and the Matthew account of Herod's political involvement gives no glory to kings. He has exalted the humble and meek, beginning with the story of his arrival. God is *for* man—that is part of the Christmas message. The man in the street dimly suspects that this is so, but he is often surprised to discover that the church is or tries to be for him, too. Christmas preaching is the announcement of the joy-making news that God is for man, excluding only those who find common humanity too common. Christmas preaching has as part of its goal the evocation of the response: "Glory to God in the highest," in a partnership of men and angels. Romans 8 could be useful supplementary material for a meditation along those lines.

The First Sunday after Christmas

Lutheran	*Roman Catholic*	*Episcopal*	*Pres./UCC/Chr.*	*Methodist/COC*
Isa. 63:7-9	Eccl. 3:2-6, 12-14	Isa. 60:13-21	Eccl. 3:1-9	Eccl. 3:1-9, 14-
Gal. 4:4-7	Col. 3:12-21	Gal. 4:4-7	Col. 3:12-17	Col. 3:12-21
Matt. 2:13-15, 19-23	Matt. 2:13-15, 19-23	John 1:1-18	Matt. 2:13-15, 19-23	Matt. 2:13-15,

EXEGESIS

First Lesson: Isa. 63:7-9. This selection is the introduction of a much larger composition, which includes 63:7—64:12. This piece is classified as a "psalm of lamentation," a literary type of which the book of Psalms contains examples in abundance. It is a common feature of this type that the lamentation and petition are preceded by a recital of the saving deeds of Yahweh in the past. This selection is such a recital. It carries on the characteristic Advent-Nativity theme of the coming of the Lord in salvation.

The first sentence (v. 7) is prolix even for late Hebrew poetry, and the text shows signs of expansion. The author uses the word "steadfast love" (Authorized Version "loving-kindness") in the plural to signify a deed of steadfast love. It is these which he wishes to recount and does through vv. 10-14; "recount" is literally "bring to mind." In Hebrew to remember is to make present the past object of memory. The prolixity of the rest of the sentence is the result of a generous use of commonplaces.

In v. 8 the author recalls the language of the covenant (Exod. 19:5, often echoed in the Pentateuch, Psalms and prophets). "Deal falsely" or "betray" became a common word in some of the prophets; it means infidelity to one's pledged word. It is opposed to the Hebrew *'emet*, the word which means both truth and fidelity. The trust which Yahweh places in his people is here represented as more than slightly naive. The result of this trust is that he became their savior—a key word in many of the NT readings for this season. The saving acts of Yahweh are specified in the recital which follows, vv. 10-14.

V. 9 is textually doubtful, and a preferable translation is: "In all their affliction it was no emissary nor messenger; it was his presence which saved them." This verse is possibly the earliest biblical example of a type of circumlocution for the deity which became common in postbiblical Judaism, although one should not ascribe to this author precisely the thought patterns of postbiblical Judaism. Reverence, it is commonly thought, led later rabbis to avoid the divine name and to use such titles as the name, the heavens, the word, the presence, and a large number of similar titles which avoided a direct mention of the deity. This author shows no such exaggerated reverence in the use of the divine name. But the earliest intermediary was the messenger of Yahweh, "the angel," who appears even in early literature as a substitute for Yahweh either in speech or in action. Angels, for instance, announce the fall of Sodom and deliver Lot; but Yahweh himself sends fire and brimstone upon the cities (Gen. 19). This prophet asserts that Yahweh did not act through such intermediaries in the saving acts of the exodus but acted directly. It was his "presence," literally his "face." The author's effort to express this direct action has been lost in the RSV rendering of this passage. The author is, of course, no more than faithful to the exodus narratives of Exod.-Num., in which no angels are active. The "face" of Yahweh, meaning himself, is affirmed to go with the Israelites in Exod. 33:14; Deut. 4:37. The author seems to be maintaining the older view of the presence and direct action of Yahweh against the more recent practice of speaking of intermediaries.

Strangely enough the very word "face," by which the author attempts to express directness, became in later Judaism one of the circumlocutions by which speaking of the presence and direct action of Yahweh was avoided. The author completes his statement of the direct aid rendered by Yahweh by the figure of carrying, found also in Exod. 19:4; Deut. 1:31; 32:11; Isa. 46:4.

Second Lesson: Gal. 4:4-7. This reading, like any reading taken out of Galatians, is difficult; we should at least set it in context. Paul's basic

thesis in Galatians is that Christians are free of the Law. He contrasts
their condition as children, who are free even if they do not have unre-
stricted use of their freedom, with the condition of slaves. The Jews and
Judaizing Christians who preach submission to the Law are slaves proclaiming slavery. Christian freedom has been achieved by the Son, who
can communicate freedom because he is free. The reading, however, was
not selected for this background but because of its allusion to the birth
of the Son.

"The fullness of time" (v. 4) does not refer to a hidden schedule of
predestination. Paul means that nothing happens by chance, and that
this event was brought about by God at the moment which he knows to
be best. The pre-existence of the Son is implied rather clearly; and the
fact that Paul does not argue the point or dwell upon it at any length
shows that he assumes that his readers know what he means. His emphasis falls upon the statement that the Son was a man and that he was
a Jew. It is doubtful that "born of a woman" carries any implication of
the virgin birth, since the phrase refers to a normal natural process.
Every Jewish male was "born under the Law," for Judaism was trans-
mitted through the mother. It is rather odd that Paul does not mention
circumcision, the ritual by which the obligation of observing the Law
was imposed. Some interpreters suppose that Paul, who is arguing against
the need of circumcision, did not wish to complicate his argument by
mentioning that Jesus was circumcised.

The humanity and the Judaism of Jesus are based on Paul's belief that
the redeemer must share the conditions from which he redeems others.
In the same way, Paul has argued earlier (3:10-14) that Jesus had to be
cursed in order to liberate men from the curse of the Law. Paul uses the
figure of purchasing slaves (the literal meaning of "redeem"). Many interpreters suggest that he is thinking of the Hellenistic practice by which
the slave deposited the price of his freedom (which he had earned) in a
temple; he thus became the slave of the god, who manumitted him.
Perhaps, but liberation from slavery did not mean adoption into a family;
and it is important for Paul that this is what liberation means. The Son
shares the conditions of those whom he liberates in order that they may
share the conditions of his freedom. It is obvious that Israelite law in the
OT contains no provision for adoption, and the practice is mentioned
only twice. Paul must be drawing his figure from Hellenistic and Roman
law; in the world of his time that practice was extremely common. Possibly he may refer more precisely to the practice of the adoption of a
slave by childless couples in order to provide for their old age, for he
insists that with sonship there goes heirship. The adopted son has the

full rights of sonship; he is not, as the Judaizers suggest, only halfway into the house.

The first thing the adopted sons receive is the spirit of the Son. The use of this phrase rather than the biblical "spirit of God" is not merely casual. A charismatic impulse of an entirely new kind enters the world when the Son enters it. The spirit inspires to speak, and the first word of the adopted son is the first word of the child who learns to speak: "Father." These are the words attributed to Jesus in Gethsemane (Mark 14:36; the Aramaic word *Abba* does not appear in Matthew and Luke). Galatians, however, is older than Mark (although not necessarily older than the passion narrative). Most interpreters believe that the phrase was an early cultic formula in Gentile communities; Palestinian communities would not need to add "Father." Paul makes the formula a charismatic attestation of Christian freedom.

Gospel: Matt. 2:13-15, 19-23. Matthew's story of the Magi, unknown to Luke, is an imaginative theological expansion of faith in Jesus as Messiah, with no authentic memory of the events and a generous use of the OT. The atrocity ascribed to Herod the Great is unknown to any other ancient source, and while it is in harmony with his character as Josephus presented it, there is no satisfactory explanation of the silence of Josephus and others. This reading omits this grisly episode (vv. 16-18). It also omits the adoration of the Magi, another detail which presents insoluble problems to the historian. It is, however, readily understood as a statement of Matthew's thesis that the Messiah, unrecognized by the Jews, his own people (as in 2:4-6), was recognized by the Gentiles who found him not in the Scriptures but in astrology. In fact, what this selection retains of the chapter is hardly more than an explanation of why Jesus was known as Jesus of Nazareth and not as Jesus of Bethlehem. Luke has a different explanation.

As in Matt. 1, the actions of Joseph are guided by dream revelations throughout. Whether this detail of the legend was based on an actual sojourn of the family in Egypt simply cannot be determined. If they were in Egypt, it cannot have been for the reasons given in the narrative. It is clear that Matthew means to show that the descent of Jacob into Egypt was a type of the descent of the Messiah into Egypt. The text of Hos. 11:1, quoted in 2:15, suits Matthew's typology better than any of the numerous texts referring to the exodus which he could have quoted; for only in this text is the exodus from Egypt combined with the designation of Israel as "son." The text is a good example of "fulfillment" by verbal association, and its use follows the rabbinical principle of exegesis that everything in the sacred text has meaning—in fact, that its meaning is inexhaustible.

Since by modern reckoning Herod died in 4 B.C., there is a superficial difficulty of chronology; but no one believes that the sixth century monk to whom we owe our era calculated the birth of Jesus correctly. It is important to recall that Matthew and Luke did not know it either. Herod could have died after the birth of Jesus. If it were proved that he did, it would not establish Matt. 2 as historical; it would merely remove one difficulty. Matthew knew Archelaus as the successor of Herod appointed by the Romans.

Matthew's non-text in v. 23 is the most celebrated example of his "fulfillment" text. The verse does not occur in the OT nor is the town of Nazareth mentioned in the OT, the Talmud, or the Midrash. Interpreters generally believe that Matthew combined two texts: Isa. 11:1, "There shall come forth a shoot" (*neser*) and Judg. 13:5, "The boy (Samson) shall be called a Nazirite" (a consecrated state described in Num. 6:1-21).

Here once again we are confronted with the fulfillment text which is based on verbal association—indeed, on mere verbal assonance. Somewhere in the OT the unexpected emergence of the Messiah from Nazareth had to be predicted, however cryptic the prediction might be. This is what the Christian scribes found. The principle, as we have said, was that the meaning of the text was inexhaustible.

HOMILETICAL INTERPRETATION

With the chief celebration of Christmas past, it is appropriate in the following weeks to ponder in our hearts, like Mary, the saving acts of God which we have witnessed. Today's propers could be brought together in a sermon on the theme of freedom. The fact or doctrine is defined in the Second Lesson, the cost is implied in the Gospel and the motivation is movingly stated in the First Lesson. Or the eternal purpose of God could be traced through its Old and New Testament expression in the respective lessons, using the Gospel to meditate on the role of Providence in shaping events towards their ultimate fulfillment. In any correlation of the readings, it will be clear that it is God who acts within history on man's behalf. Saving "coincidences" from man's perspective are part of God's design, a design that finds its center in the events that describe the gift of God's Son for and to mankind.

The First Lesson invites meditation on the immanence of God. Technology and science make belief in God's immanence more difficult, perhaps, but a false sophistication on the part of Christians has been even more responsible for the inability of many to be thankful to the Giver of goodness and life. The emphasis on and enjoyment of praise and thanksgiving on the part of charismatics is a reminder to the conventional church that it has forgotten the simplicity of faith: God leads, defends and feeds his children, and not by intermediaries, either. He comes himself. How he comes, today's Second Lesson and subsequent lessons make clear. Sonship (and the freedom of sons) is the theme of the Second Lesson. The theme is important. Modern man tends to overemphasize terms like self-realization and self-fulfillment as if personhood were enhanced by egocentric acts, self-centered planning or hostility toward authority. Galatians approaches the same theme a different way. God redeems man from slavery and offers him a share in the management of creation and in creation's riches. Not slaves but sons, is the good news brought by Christ.

A sermon on sonship has a bearing on liturgies, polity, and decision-making in the church, and an equal relevance to questions of personal maturity and social worth in the general society. If God invites us to the intimacy of "Abba" as a term of address, should not our liturgies express some alternative to abject humility before the divine grandeur? Is there no place to acknowledge that Christ has said: "I no longer call you servants; I call you friends"? If God trusts all mankind with the privileges and responsibilities of sonship, is there any justification for withholding all orders in the church from a share in decision-making? Should we not challenge the self-fulfillment image with the concept of sonship? The latter includes a wider idea of fulfillment and sets it in a social context. Socially, there is a world of difference between giving handouts to an "unfortunate" and helping in the liberation of an oppressed adopted son of the living God. If God chooses to abandon the perfectly reasonable classification of servant in order to reclassify us as sons and heirs, a corresponding shift in the philosophy of world order seems to be needed.

Freedom is another explosive theme of the Second Lesson. Liberation is a much-quoted word today, usually in a legitimate context. Too much of our personal and social living has been bound. Liberation theology as expressed by Reubem Alves or some of the black theologians should be heard and evaluated by all who are concerned with the freedom with which Christ has made us free. The church has stressed freedom from sin almost to the exclusion of the other freedoms enumerated in the NT. Freedom from Law in order to enjoy the spontaneous creativity and communion in the Spirit is a Pauline theme. So is freedom from the domination of principalities and powers; freedom from fate. Freedom from the tyranny of death is the great Easter theme. There are others.

Freedom is achieved by God on man's behalf. If that Christian affirmation clashes with contemporary political experience that freedom is taken rather than granted, remember that, first, man is not gaining his freedom from God (who has always been for it) but from the accidents of birth and the consequences of sin that make up fate, and second, freedom was achieved by the Man, Jesus Christ, in whom his Father worked. God's respect for man's dignity included the self-emptying involved in the incarnation.

The preacher's preparation for a sermon on freedom as taught in Galatians, requires a review of the argument of the whole epistle. Note the exegetical comments and take time to trace the argument through the Pauline reasoning and analogies. In this day all Christian readers will share Luther's delight in the promise for mankind that Galatians holds out.

Freedom is achieved by God, but Paul would agree that eternal vigilance is the price of freedom, spiritual as well as temporal. A sermon on freedom includes the exhortation to choose the covenant of promise rather than of law, and to stand firm in the freedom received (4:21-5:1). This side of Christ's coming bondage is not inevitable, it is therefore in some measure chosen.

Reference was made earlier to liberation theology as such. Each reader must decide the theological nuances for himself, but the times no longer permit a purely personal and eschatological approach to salvation, except at the cost of consenting to the repression of the have nots, those who resent being exploited for the comfort of those who are further advanced along the road of technology than themselves. Only a church content to be a chaplaincy to those who have arrived can deny the revolutionary character of the incarnation. Having affirmed the promise of freedom and fulfillment with its political implications included, the church is free (and only then) to maintain her witness to love, non-violence and meekness in the pursuit of a dignity which is God's will for and God's gift to all.

The flight into Egypt and the return to Nazareth and obscurity is a story which invites the use of reverent imagination and contemporary analogies. Who, today, can imagine waiting thirty years for the initiation of an enthusiastically announced project? Who has the faith to hold the Christmas story, St. Stephen's martyrdom, and the Holy Innocents' story in focus? Yet Christmas without Easter is not the Christian revelation. Art and good theology meet in the warning that the hope and innocence focused in the vulnerable Son of man are threatened by the forces of evil from the first announcement of his presence until the end of time. Threatened, but never overcome.

Some good ideas for our national life, some self-sacrificing qualities in marriage, some aspects of neighborliness, are regularly stepped on, but they do not die, and in the long run they win.

With a sophisticated congregation and a preacher who accepts the contemporary assumptions about the legendary character of the birth narratives, this Sunday would be a possible time to develop the Gospel themes through the art of story-tellers. It would be equally appropriate in a totally different theological climate to make the dogmatic assertions and explanations inappropriate to Christmas Day. The criteria for judging the worth of either sermon is its faithfulness to the Word: made flesh, and proclaiming the sonship of former slaves.

Meditation on the "hidden years" of Christ's life is also suggested by today's Gospel. Ripening, growing in wisdom and experience, waiting for the NOW of God's timing are part of the formation of the whole person. So are occasional retreats, withdrawal for prayer, rest and self-examination. How much of our Lord's bearing and presence were the result of the years of unobserved growth in the knowledge and the doing of his Father's will?

Obscurity need not be unproductive, obviously. Perhaps that is an insight for the preacher as much as for those whom he addresses. The Little Brothers (and Sisters) of Jesus founded by Charles de Foucauld are devoted to the Nazareth years, the hidden years, in their spirituality. They eschew authority, take only humble jobs, determined to be *little* brother to even the most lowly in the spirit of the self-effacing years of our Lord's life. Material by their leader, Rene Voillaume, and by Carlo Caretto can be found in English. It may be that their model has new freshness for an age disillusioned by the promises of both Caesar and mammon. A search of the OT and NT for evidence of God's use of the small and weak things to great ends would be salutary to both preacher and (eventually) hearers. Gideon, Isaiah, Jeremiah, Amos, Israel itself, the Suffering Servant, the Remnant and other OT themes lead into the picture of the Son of man, the humble twelve, and all the imagery of the manger and shepherds, adoring the Child who as an adult would have no place to lay his head.

The Name of Jesus (January 1)

Lutheran	Roman Catholic	Episcopal	Pres. / UCC / Chr.
Num. 6:22–27	Num. 6:22–27	Isa. 9:2–4, 6–7	Deut. 8:1–10
Rom. 1:1–7	Gal. 4:4–7	Rom. 1:1–7	Rev. 21:1–7
Luke 2:21	Luke 2:16–21	Luke 2:15–21	Matt. 25:15–23

EXEGESIS

First Lesson: Num. 6:22-27. This formula, known as the priestly blessing, is preserved in the Priestly source of the Pentateuch (P). Most commentators, however, believe that it is a liturgical formula far older than P. To bless is to communicate life, and thus in the OT Yahweh alone can bless. Men bless by invoking Yahweh and asking him to bless. Such a blessing is especially effective when it is uttered by a person possessed of authority, such as the priest, the king, or the head of a family. The authority of such persons is that they can speak in the name of a group. Thus blessing is not a peculiarly priestly function. The patriarchs bless their families (Gen. 48:15-16, for example), and kings bless their people (2 Sam. 6:20; 1 Kings 8:14, 55). The blessing becomes a priestly act as the role of the priest as mediator is broadened; he is thought to enjoy a peculiar power with the deity, while the king or the patriarch simply stands before the deity as the head of a group. Blessings may have the impersonal formula, "Blessed be . . .", or, as in the present passage, the personal formula, "May Yahweh bless . . .".

The priestly blessing has three lines which are balanced without being rigidly metrical; the difference is not apparent in translation. The divine name is repeated three times, each time in the second position in the line. In each line the divine name is the subject of two jussive verbs. Somewhat strangely the blessing is concerned entirely with the favorable attitude of Yahweh and not with particular objects of blessing such as long life, prosperity, fertility, or victory (see, for example, the blessing of Joseph, Gen. 49:22-26).

The first pair of words asks Yahweh to bless and to keep Israel; both of these verbs belong to the conventional language of Israelite prayer and have passed into the conventional language of prayer in English. The second pair contains an anthropomorphic symbol of the disposition expressed in the second verb. The shining face which is a sign of a favorable disposition is again a part of the conventional language of Israelite prayer (see Ps. 31:16; 80:3, 17, 19). Some commentators appeal to the light of the sun as the reality behind this figure. The "graciousness" expressed by the shining face is frequently ascribed to Yahweh as his habitual disposition towards petitioners, which can be changed to anger by misconduct. The third pair again uses the anthropomorphic figure of the face. To "lift the face" towards someone is to look favorably upon him; displeasure is shown by the averted face or the face which "falls" (Gen. 4:5-6). The goods which are hoped for as a result of blessing are summed up in the word "peace," general well-being and security.

V. 27 furnishes the handle by which this passage is attached into the liturgy at this point. "To put the name" upon some one is not only to invoke the name in prayer or in blessing; it is also to put the name as the name of the owner, who is responsible for the defense of his property. Thus Israel is the people of Yahweh, and the new Israel is the people of Jesus. Both old and new Israel are said to have been purchased or "redeemed" by him who owns them.

Second Lesson: Rom. 1:1-7. See the exegesis of the Second Lesson for the Fourth Sunday in Advent.

Gospel: Luke 2:21. Circumcision, performed one week after the birth of the male infant, was an ancient rite of initiation. There is no history of its origins among the Israelites, and no certainty about its antiquity. There is not even assurance about the symbolism of the rite. Where it was and is practiced among other peoples, it is commonly a rite of initiation into adult manhood, practiced at the age of puberty. This symbolism does not appear in Judaism; it is a rite of initiation into a religious group. That this group is exclusively male is seen in other practices such as the minimum number of ten adult males required for synagogue worship, the *minyan.* The effect of the rite is to make the person subject to the obligations of the Law.

This verse and Luke 1:59 are major pieces of evidence for the practice of conferring the name at circumcision in NT times. OT passages which allude to the conferring of a name suggest that it was done at birth. The name "Jesus" is the English version of the Greek version of the Aramaic version of a Hebrew name. In Aramaic the pronunciation would be Yeshua; there are traces in the Talmud of an abbreviated form Yeshu which seems to have been a code word for an abusive designation of Jesus. The Hebrew name is Joshua, shortened from Jehoshua, borne by the hero of the book of Joshua. Styles of names given to children do change something like styles of clothing, and the name Yeshua was quite common in Palestine in NT times. Matt. 1:21 plays upon the meaning of the name, "Yahweh is salvation." Most Hebrew names are a sentence, usually a prayer. The absence of this interpretation leads one to wonder whether the Gentile Luke knew the meaning of the name. In Matt. 1:21 the name is explained as one who saves his people from their sins. This is not an OT phrase; in the OT salvation has a definite "this world" content. Salvation from sin becomes in the NT the unique salvation wrought by Jesus. Thus the interpretation of the name is another affirmation of a non-political and non-secular messiahship.

By the time Matthew and Luke wrote their Gospels the early church had already developed its theology of the name of Jesus, which is reflected in their accounts of the conferring of the name. The early church did not say that Jesus Christ is God; they reserved this title for the Father. But they spoke of the name of Jesus in the same way in which the OT books spoke of the name of Yahweh. It is a personal name by which diseases are healed and demons are exorcised, sins are forgiven and holiness is conferred. There is no other name by which men can be saved (Acts 4:12). It is a name exalted above every other name (Phil. 2:9-11); by saying this Paul does the best he can with his linguistic resources to distinguish Jesus from every other being besides the Father. Christians are known as those who invoke the name of Jesus and are called by his name. In biblical language to be called by the name of another is to belong to him. To proclaim the gospel is the same thing as proclaiming the name of Jesus (so, for example, in Acts 5:40; 8:12; 9:15). In John 3:18 the Christian faith is compendiously defined as faith in the name of Jesus. The disciples must suffer in the name of Jesus. Paul said that one could not say "Jesus is Lord" except by a charismatic impulse of the spirit (1 Cor. 12:3).

In many of these uses we encounter the biblical use of the "name" as signifying the person. At the same time, the power which is attributed to the person is also attributed to the name. The Jewish background of the NT imposed certain linguistic restraints upon its writers. In the theology of the name they attempt to express their belief that Jesus and the Father share a level of being which is shared by no one else.

HOMILETICAL INTERPRETATION

Probably the Feast of the Name of Jesus will not carry as much religious weight in people's thinking as New Year's Day despite the efforts of the church to focus the thoughts of worshipers on salvation history rather than the calendar. There is a legitimate instinct to face the calendar year—the year which makes us older and in which births and deaths are recorded, the year by which we are taxed—in a spirit of penitence, prayer and hope. It will not be hard to do justice to the primary meaning of today's pericopes while applying them to the unfolding year. If a sermon on "time" has not been preached during Advent today's propers (especially the Second Lesson chosen by Presbyterians and UCC) provide excellent material.

Note that the Lutherans use Rom. 1:1-7 already exegeted for Advent IV as today's Second Lesson. The exegetical and homiletical notes have already commented on Gal. 4:4-7 (the Roman Catholic propers) for today. Homiletical comments on Rev. 21:1-7 (the Presbyterian and UCC lessons) are included here.

The OT blessing read in today's First Lesson and used liturgically by some churches should have far wider use than it presently does. As indicated in the exegesis, blessing is the privilege and prerogative of parents, chiefs, heads, and all others who are recognized as the focus of a group. Some Europeans assemble on New Year's Day to be blessed by the grandfather or great grandfather. It is a powerful form of Christian education to see four generations, sometimes, involved in giving or receiving the blessing. A sermon on the meaning of blessing should involve some OT research on the concept of the "sharing of soul" involved. There are good articles available in dictionaries or encyclopedias of religion under the heading of blessing, name, soul, etc. A blessing is more than a pious wish. It is a conferral; something is actually given and actually received.

The exchange of the peace, now practiced in several of the churches, is a related practice. It would not be objected to as an interruption of the services if it were considered as the time when God's peace given to each is exchanged among all in preparation for the subsequent breaking of bread together.

God's blessing on his people as they prepare for the events of the coming year, the grace and peace of Christ with which the Second Lesson (Lutheran and Episcopal lectionary) ends, and our meditation on them, like the shepherds and like Mary, are the components of a New Year's meditation on the riches of Christian faith and Christian resources, centering in the gift of God through the incarnation of Jesus Christ.

Presbyterian and UCC congregations will find the vision of the new Jerusalem and of Christ as Alpha and Omega a very apt accompaniment of the OT and Gospel selections for a New Year's Day sermon. The events of Christmas are our basis for hope in the coming year and they are our assurance that the vision of ultimate life and peace is not an illusion but rather a foretaste and foresight of the eternal purpose of God. The statement that "the dwelling of God is with men" recalls the name Emmanuel: God with us, and joins Christmas and the ultimate Kingdom in one experience and hope.

Pain, sorrow and death are overcome in the holy city: God will wipe away every tear from the eyes of his people. The Advent OT lessons and the Christian passion to share, following the teaching and example of Christ, make it clear that the Kingdom calls for equity, justice and freedom from want. Here the message is that God gives us himself, the ultimately satisfying gift. The Gospel selection for Presbyterians and UCC corrects any possible imbalance inferred from the Second Lesson. However, our ˉhuman participation in the Kingdom is to be judged on the basis of our treatment of the needy.

A sermon on the name of Jesus following the Lutheran and Episcopal pericopes invites contemplation both of the name "Jesus" and the title "Son of God." By extension "Son of man," "Emmanuel," "King of Kings," and perhaps "Man of Sorrows" and other biblical titles ascribed to our Lord might be considered. Reference was made earlier to the title "Jesus Christ our Lord" as a subject for a teaching sermon, or one of quiet thanksgiving. Shepherd, brother, friend, way, truth, life are also biblical concepts. Litanies of names and titles have sometimes been lovingly strung together. It might be feasible in some places to construct a prayer-dialogue in which meditation on a name or title is followed by invocation of Christ by that name. At any rate, a sermon on the name of Jesus may call some preachers to that kind of prayerful meditation.

The exegetical notes suggest the kind of saving power the church has experienced in contact with Jesus, the Lord. They also suggest the power of the name as identified with the person. Preaching on the name of Jesus, therefore, involves consideration of man's need, God's response in Christ, and man's appropriation and use of the power of Jesus as his agent and in his spirit.

Man's state involves both material and spiritual bondage. Saving us involves changes both in the environment and in our inner attitude and value systems. It is easy to see how obedience to Christ makes measurable changes in community attitude and hence in the environment. It is harder to speculate on what actual change in the physical creation itself may have been achieved by the presence within it of the power that created it. Meditation and reading by the preacher on the cosmic dimension of Christ's ministry are essential to the preparation of a sermon on salvation of any depth. It is perhaps not entirely fanciful and sentimental that so many Christmas stories involve some response on the part of animals, or the appearance of a Christmas rose, or the Epiphany star itself. Unsophisticated believers sense the cosmic aspect of Christ's com-

ing and fill in conjectural ideas in the absence of more thoughtful theological statements.

The cosmic deliverance includes defeat of the "powers" that oppress
us. Whether these are considered to be personal malevolent beings, or a
collective expression of the sinful and negative inner life of individuals
that adds up to a sum of evil greater than its parts, makes little difference. We are often bound by a "spirit of the age" which makes whole
constructive trends of thinking impossible except by outside intervention.
Jesus was that intervention at Christmas. The presence of Jesus Christ
and the invocation of Jesus Christ make that kind of saving intervention
always possible. That is the truth which lies behind exorcism. Christians
are either unaware of or reluctant to use the power of God for salvation
to everyone who believes.

Deliverance from death, from sin, from isolation, is the Easter work of
salvation. We tell the story but we seldom expect to experience the
power. First century Christians documented the resurrection in part by
the testimony of the apostles, but much more by their personal knowledge of the risen Christ. Today the churches that are growing are the
ones in which Christians witness to their own changed lives by the intervention of Jesus Christ and who in turn invoke the name and power
of Jesus on behalf of others. It is curious that at a time when the
churches whose liturgical practice has stressed the exercise of Christ's
spiritual authority for changing lives are revising their rites in a rational
and "relevant" way, the "fringe" churches are reviving the ancient rites
and discipline, although sometimes in a spur of the moment fashion.
Many interpretations are possible. There is a good sermon and a useful
one in the use of these passages towards that end. The sermon will probably be more profound if it neither uncritically endorses nor unsympa-
thetically condemns the new movement. Those most in position to criti-
cize are those who already demonstrate familiarity with power to save.

Adam named the creatures of creation and so signified his dominion
over them in the Genesis account. We bear the name of Jesus and we
are his people. For eternal good and perhaps some temporal ill our for-
tunes are identified with his. When he is popular we are respected. When
he is despised so are we, as publicly recognized Christians. Today there
is a new phenomenon at work: the rejection and ridicule of the church
as an institution whose style is contrary to that of the name she invokes.
While the accusations are not all true, the basic insistence that the farther the institution gets from Bethlehem, the farther it gets from the
power-bringing presence of Christ must be considered. Not the basilicas
in the Holy Land but the fields, oases, lakes and hills act as reminders of

the Lord's presence. Currently the catacombs in Rome speak more elo-
quently of Christian vocation and Christian unity than St. Peter's. Those
who minister among outward signs of splendor today may be called to
do so, but they must remember that the signs which once seemed to
confirm their preaching are read today as contradictions. If Christians
are ready to meet the world's demands that they match the humility of
Jesus, they may find it easier to exercise his power.

The Hymnal may be a help in sermon preparation for this day. The
pietist tradition in each of the ethnic groups, the hymnology of the
Roman Catholic mystics, the more objective hymns written for liturgical
use, and St. Patrick's Breastplate ("I bind unto myself, today, the strong
Name of the Trinity") provide material which used after the sermon may
clinch the point.

Basically, of course, the Christmas season continues another week
despite its commercial abandonment. It would be unfortunate if the
churches were to give in totally to the pressure to merge Advent and
Christmas into one rather hectic time. The post-Christmas services provide time to ponder and to wonder and to choose, and to continue to
sing the quieter Christmas hymns.

The Second Sunday after Christmas

Lutheran	Roman Catholic	Episcopal	Pres./UCC/Chr.	Methodist/COCU
Isa. 61:10-62:3	Eccl. 24:1-2, 8-12	Isa. 61:10-62:3	Prov. 8:22-31	Isa. 61:10-62:3
Eph. 1:3-6, 15-18	Eph. 1:3-6, 15-18	Eph. 1:3-6, 15-18	Eph. 1:15-23	Eph. 1:3-6, 15-18
John 1:1-18	John 1:1-18	Matt. 2:13-15, 19-23	John 1:1-5, 9-14	John 1:1-18

EXEGESIS

First Lesson: Isa. 61:10-62:3. This reading joins portions of two
different poems of Third Isaiah. The selection comes from Isa. 60-62, a
collection of three poems known as the Zion poems. The theme of these
poems is the restoration of Jerusalem after the exile; the language suggests that this had not yet been accomplished. More precisely, the
prophet speaks of the rebuilding of Jerusalem; the Zion poems of Second
Isaiah (49:14–55:13) speak rather of the return of the exiles and the
repopulation of Jerusalem. Some confusion is possible because of the
change of the speaker between the two poems. The "I" of 61:10-11 is
Jerusalem, for whom the prophet speaks; the "I" of 62:1 is the prophet,
and Jerusalem is the one addressed.

The rejoicing of Jerusalem is given a festive, even a cultic tone; in ancient times (and in modern as well) there were appropriate festal garments for festive occasions. These included the wearing of wreaths of flowers upon the head. The festal garments of Jerusalem are two divine attributes frequent in Second and Third Isaiah, salvation and righteousness. Both of these words have a breadth of meaning which is a problem for translators who do not like to paraphrase. Both can be rendered "victory." Since righteousness was not fully authentic unless it was proved and recognized, the word can sometimes be paraphrased as vindication. Deliverance from danger and victory over enemies are works of God which prove that he is on one's side—therefore that one is righteous. In exilic and postexilic literature the supreme work of Yahweh's righteousness—doing what he ought—was the restoration of his people from death to life. V. 11, a somewhat obscure figure, refers to the manifestation of righteousness; the saving act of Yahweh for his people will be as undeniable as the vegetation which springs from the soil.

In the words spoken by the prophet in his own person (62:1-3) he continues to play upon the same two words. The rhetorical flourish "I will not keep silence" is taken by many commentators to refer to his intercessory prayer, but this is not expressed here or elsewhere in the Zion poems. More probably he refers to his message of promise, which he intends to continue to proclaim until he sees its fulfillment. There is ample evidence in postexilic literature that the prophets who promised restoration spoke to a dull, dispirited and incredulous people. And in some respects it may be said that they overstated their case. Christian interpreters have believed that the glory of the new Jerusalem was not fulfilled until Jesus, its true savior, appeared in it and built the true new Jerusalem.

The conferring of a new name (vv. 2 and 4, the latter not included in the reading) leaves interpreters uncertain how far the prophet meant to go. A new name is demanded by a new reality. In another even more obscure passage of Third Isaiah it seems that the author meant that the new people would no longer be called Israel (65:15). In v. 4, however, the author speaks not of a new "name" strictly but of a new adjective; the old name was Jerusalem, not "Forsaken" or "Desolate." The point is of some importance in determining whether the prophet spoke of the restoration of a former reality or the creation of a new reality. His language generally seems to suggest that he thought of a new reality.

The image of the festal garment is continued with a new element. Yahweh himself will take part in the festivities, and he will wear Jeru-

salem as a festal wreath. In vv. 4-5 this festal wreath becomes the wedding wreath: the poet did not seek perfect consistency in his imagery.

Second Lesson: Eph. 1:3-6, 15-18. Whether Paul wrote Ephesians is
an unsolved problem of criticism. The reader who notices a certain
prolixity even in the translation is noticing one of the reasons for the
question. If Paul did write the letter, he used the assistance of others in
ways which he did not use in writing the letters which are surely his.
This selection is drawn somewhat violently from the introduction to the
epistle. Vv. 3-6 are taken from the thanksgiving, which is hymnic in tone
but not poetry. Vv. 15-18 are the beginning of the prayer of intercession
which continues to the end of the chapter. Both are broken off abruptly
for no obvious reason.

The thanksgiving is offered for "spiritual" blessings; this word "spiritual" does not have the rather vapid meaning which it has in modern
homiletics, but designates the blessings which come with the gift of the
Spirit. This blessing has been conferred in "the heavenly places"; here
and in the following verses the writer emphasizes that the saving acts of
God do not proceed by chance or by random experiment but by a
planned decision made "in heaven," in a region raised above contingency
and the uncertainties of human events. Thus the election of Christians
was made before creation. It is altogether doubtful that the writer had
in mind the theological excesses which have been committed in the name
of "election" and "predestination." He simply meant that God did not
make a random choice and was in no way inhibited by the existing situation. In the same way he "destined" those who are to be adopted as
sons. Adoption did not proceed independently of his will. All that happens is done "for the praise of his glorious grace." It is God's purpose to
act that his true character will be recognized. His true character is
"gracious," but he also revealed that his grace is bestowed exclusively
through "the Beloved."

The selection, as we have noticed, breaks off the thanksgiving here
and picks up the beginning of the prayer in v. 15. It seems strange that
Paul, who spent three years in the evangelization of Ephesus, should say
that he has heard of the faith and love of the Ephesians. He uses the
already pregnant Christian phrase "faith in the Lord Jesus." The love
with which faith attests genuine Christianity is shown to all the saints.
His prayer for them—at least that part of it which the selection preserves
—has a somewhat Gnostic tone. He prays that they may receive a spirit
of wisdom and revelation in knowledge, that the eyes of their heart may
be enlightened. Is this the same Paul that said he proclaimed only Christ

and him crucified (1 Cor. 2:2)? Plainly the content of the gospel has grown since Paul wrote those lines. The author of Ephesians is concerned with what he calls "the mystery," which in general is the saving plan of God. More particularly the mystery as expounded in Ephesians is the place of Christ in creation and salvation. The epistle proposes "the cosmic Christ," and it is perhaps the earliest Christian document to propose this view of Christ. It also sets forth a view of the relations of Christ to the church; and it seems to be again the earliest document to identify the church with Christ as his body. This teaching, it seems, is what the author felt could not be perceived without a charismatic spirit of wisdom and of the understanding of revelation.

Gospel: John 1:1-18. The prologue of the Gospel of John touches the Synoptic Gospels at only two points: the allusions to John the Baptist (6-8; 15) and the reference to the birth of Jesus (14). The rest of the prologue moves on a theological level which was not attempted by the Synoptics and was, we may say confidently, unknown to them. John emphasizes that the birth was the appearance in the "world" (a key word of John) of the preexistent Word. In comparison to the genealogies of Matthew and Luke, who push the antecedents of Jesus back to Abraham and Adam respectively, John pushes them back before creation. "In the beginning" (v. 1) must be deliberately intended to echo Gen. 1:1. And since the Word is anterior to creation, he must be "God." John did not intend to identify the Word with the Father; he did intend to make a distinction between the Word and creatures which no other NT writer makes so clearly.

The Word is not a creature because he shares in the work of creation. No doubt John derives this from the theology of creation of the word, which is clear in Gen. 1:1—2:4a, even though this document does use the verbs create and make. The general theme of the narrative is expressed in the refrain, "God said . . . and it happened." The cosmic function of the Son grew more important in the early church as the scope of the redemptive act was conceived in wider and wider terms until it came to be called a new creation. In John's statement of the cosmic function of the Word, he sees the Word as the agent of life. "Life" and "light" are key words in John; again he echoes the creation account of Gen. 1, in which light and life are produced by the creative word of God.

As in the Synoptic Gospels, John is precursor; but only in John's Gospel is he a witness to the light. The "light" is a creative reality like the "word," and mere man could only bear witness to both. The "true" light was the light which shone over creation in the beginning. This light shines again with the entrance of the Word into the world; a new creation is begun with the appearance of the light and the coming of the Word. John descends briefly to historical reality with the allusion to "his home" and "his own people"; but it is doubtful that he was thinking only of the Jews. It was "the world" of men which was made through him which knew him not.

The new life is birth from God. John does not use the language of adoption like Paul, but he does reserve the Greek word *hyios* for the Son, and uses the word *teknon* for the "child" of God. These are "born" of God. The incarnation of the Word is described not as a birth but as a coming. The word "flesh" removes any suspicion that the Word was not fully human; for "flesh" is the mortal and the corruptible component of man. The word "dwelt" (literally "pitched his tent"), on the other hand, could be open to misinterpretation. But the biblical background of the word echoes the dwelling of God with Israel. This allusion probably lies behind the reference to the vision of the glory of the Word; for it was in the tent that the glory of Yahweh was revealed to the Israelites (Num. 14:10). Jesus was the revelation of the glory of the Father.

The prologue closes with an antithesis between the revelation of the Law and the revelation of the Word. The Law was not "grace and truth," standard attributes of Yahweh in the OT. These attributes are not fully revealed except in Jesus Christ. Nor did the Law really make God known; it is a standard feature of OT theology that God is invisible, and, by a paradox, that the sight of him is fatal to the viewer. Only the only-begotten Son has seen him, and only he can tell of him as one who has seen him.

HOMILETICAL INTERPRETATION

Light and glory are themes that weave their way through the propers for this day. Explicitly, light figures in the First Lesson and the Gospel, and glory in the Second Lesson and Gospel, but all three are concerned with the radiance of human beings who accept the sanctifying grace of God. The glory of God in Christ is available to all who live in Christ. Christmas is the glorification of man, and Christmas makes visible the glory of God. Redeemed man is God's glory. Recall the earlier reference to David Jenkins and his use of Irenaeus' statement: "The glory of God is a living man." Righteousness is the source of the radiance in the Isaiah passage. Victorious Israel actually adorns the living God. In the Second Lesson the knowledge of God as he is revealed in the mystery of Christ is the source of glory, a knowledge that includes God's plan of salvation, the experience of redemption, and, in the passages not read, the existence of "the church, his body, the fullness of him who fills all in all." The Gospel locates the glory in Jesus Christ: creative Word, life, light, shining since before the beginning of time, now in the world, sharing that power with those who receive him.

After meditating a good while on the bits and pieces of this kaleidoscope of glory, a preacher might focus on living man—the nature of his life, the style of his life and the end of his life—to glorify God. Or one might start at the other end and preach on the splendor of God in creation, in the incarnation of Christ and in redeemed man (or the church, if more of Ephesians is used). Or one could preach on Christ, agent of creation, splendor of Israel, first of many sons of God. There is room here, too, for contemplation of the grandeur and misery of man, to borrow a splendid title from the late David E. Roberts.

One word of caution: glory cannot be ponderous, pedantic or dull. It would be better to suggest mystery than to try to explain it all, and better to help the hearers share in the enlightening experience of God's grace than to catalog the possible ways in which God reveals himself. The Epiphany of God's glory, the manifestation of light, is not through hearing the accounts of stars sighted and angels overheard, or even through detached exposition of the Prologue to John. God is manifested through the believers: their righteousness, their life, their concern for the least of God's little ones, and the numinous quality of their worship. If God's glory does not shine out everywhere it is because we do not excel, usually, in any of those qualities. But sometimes the splendor breaks through, and preaching has a place in preparing the way.

It is unlikely that one would choose the OT alone as the basis of a sermon in the light of the importance of the Gospel in the Christian tradition. Still, the exegetical notes remind us that prophets are called to inspire the dispirited and open their hearts to new vocations under new names. The theme is timely. The purpose of God unfolding age by age is spelled out or implied in all three lessons and the historical setting of postexilic Israel is a suggestive base from which to begin. Many Christians are mourning over lost institutional wealth, prestige, size, and splendor of language and art. To know that God could use the remnant of Israel to bring forth a new and more splendid revelation of himself because they were willing to become once more a trusting pilgrim people, is to be better prepared to celebrate the mystery of sonship and our own brand of venturing into the unknown.

The Second Lesson invites a consideration of spiritual blessings. Very substantial are the spiritual blessings described in our incarnational theology. A destiny of sonship to God decided upon before the creation, effected in Christ and effective forever, forgiveness of sins, a part in uniting (reconciling) all things through Christ, an appreciation of the eventual inheritance and a living, working hope are a sound basis for stable faith and consistent action. The action, note, is God's. Experience and feeling are present but they are not the basis of confidence. Security is in God alone.

If the Second Lesson is chosen as the basis of the sermon, it would be wise to read and base the preaching on 1:15-23, not 1:15-18. It is hard to trust the judgment of the scholars who gave us the lectionary in this instance. The reference to power in verse 19 has obvious rapport with the Gospel for the day and should be noted.

Evangelistic use of the Second Lesson, or a plea for more experiential faith is an appropriate way to end the Christmas season. God has acted: now believers pray that the eyes of men's hearts may be enlightened so that they may appropriate and share the gift and the blessings received. The opening of men's eyes is a gift, a gift to be prayed for on behalf of others by those who have already seen the light; the light of Christ.

The Gospel is dear to the Catholic, Reformed, and Lutheran traditions alike as a theological and devotional summary of the drama of redemption. It defines Christ in pre-historical terms: keynote of Christian theology, but a meeting-place, too, for those who do not know the historical Jesus but do appear to be in relation to the creative Word, the light that enlightens every man, the light of creation. Every Christmas season calls for a sermon on the cosmic Christ, not in terms that are a stumbling-block for those who cannot believe, but just the opposite, an encouragement to recognize in more personal terms the concepts made flesh, the light and word and life already encountered. This is a day to make clear how much bigger Jesus Christ the Lord is than all the statements about him, and to welcome the agnostic fellow-travelers to share as much of our joy as their consciences will allow. We have absolutely nothing to lose. In that connection we might explicitly repent of our efforts to confine Christ to manageable definitions and local customs. In the context of the Prologue to John, Christian mind-expansion in the contemplation of the scope of the person and work of Jesus Christ is inevitable.

The Gospel is the basis for an evangelistic sermon. Christ is in his world, but men do not recognize him. (Why not?) Those who do receive him are given power to become God's sons. Receiving him is comparable to the enlightenment for which the writer of Ephesians prays. Receiving him or believing in his name are ideas worthy of individual or corporate research. A theology of conversion, of the church, of baptism, is involved.

The consequences of receiving Christ are described in the Second Lesson and the righteousness imparted and experienced can be described in the imagery of the First Lesson.

"Power to become" is another theme to develop. That was the promise to creation marred by sin. Limited by creation to his place in the natural order, to becoming what genes and chromosomes might make him, man was further limited by sin to the point of bondage. Still the image of God within made him unsatisfied with his fate. Now the word and the light of creation have come to us again, personally, and in the person of Jesus Christ, to give us power to become the children of God. Note that we are not, this side of the fall, children of God by creation, but by deliberate and individual redemption. The redemption includes freedom from the Law and the substitution of grace and truth for precept and code.

There is a sermon here, and in conjunction with the Second Lesson, on sonship. Christian humanism is more audacious by far than secular humanism. Far from the eighteenth and early nineteenth century conflict that saw man's dignity as an infringement on God's sovereignty, biblical Christianity sees God as planning from the beginning to elevate man to partnership in creation, to partnership in the continuing work of redemption and reconciliation, and to a destiny in and with Christ at God's right hand, the place of ultimate power. It doesn't happen automatically: sonship must be accepted. But it is a gift, not an achievement. We start there, in baptism, and we may, if we will, go on from there.

The antithesis between law and grace can be worked out from today's lessons. Chiefly, the knowledge that God is the one who gives the power that liberates, and that he does it in Christ, is the message that has to be translated into everyday terms. The Prologue to John indicates that a liberating word may come from any direction, from any agent, but that if it brings power to become a child of God, we know the name that gives it power. Note, by reference to the OT, that freedom from the Law does not mean freedom from responsible behavior or righteousness. It is the substitution of power to become, power to be, what God intends man to be. In that context, Christian sex morality, Christian marriage, financial honesty, truthfulness can all be seen as a consequence of beholding the glory of God in the face of Jesus Christ, and reflecting some of it ourselves. We become like what we admire and contemplate.

Few congregations can take their theology straight, but few would be anything but grateful for the preaching of these truths in understandable analogies. Moralism and spiritual uplift have been pretty widely rejected, but there is a hunger for righteousness and spiritual wisdom. No other duty or privilege is more important than the ministry of the word. It takes a great deal of time for preparation, and the claim on the preacher is not as insistent as the telephone, the doorbell and the mail. But the source of the claim is the Word who dwells with us though he was and is beyond all words and worlds.